THE MISANDRIST

by Lisa Carroll

The Misandrist was first performed at
Arcola Theatre, London, on 10 May 2023,
presented by Metal Rabbit Productions

by Lisa Carroll

Rachel	Elf Lyons
Nick	Nicholas Armfield
Director	Bethany Pitts
Set and Costume Designer	Cara Evans
Lighting Designer	Peter Small
Sound Designer	Dominic Brennan
Intimacy and Movement Director	Louise Kempton
Casting Director	Martin Poile
Costume Supervisor	Trynity Silk
Executive Producer	George Warren
Associate Producers	Simon Paris and Oli Seymour
Production Manager	Andreas Ayling
Company Stage Manager	Maja Lach
Assistant Stage Manager	Adam Maxey

Elf Lyons
Rachel

Elf Lyons is an award-winning comedian and theatre-maker. Past solo shows include: *Raven* (Soho and Leicester Square Theatre); *Talks Dirty* (Soho Theatre); *Love Songs to Guinea Pigs* (VAULT Festival, Soho Theatre); *ChiffChaff* (Pleasance, Omnibus Theatre) and *Swan* (Edinburgh Fringe, Fringe World Perth, Adelaide Fringe and Soho Theatre). Theatre shows include: *Duffy & Elf: Heist* (Soho Theatre); *Unlikely Darlings* (VAULT Festival); *Gorgon: A Horror Story* (VAULT Festival) and *Medusa* (Nuffield Theatre, Southampton). Award nominations for her work have included the Edinburgh Comedy Award for Best Show at the Edinburgh Fringe, the Malcolm Hardee Award for Comic Originality, British Comedy Guide's Comedians Choice Award, Fringe World Perth's Best Comedy Show and Adelaide Fringe's Pick of the Fringe. Elf teaches clowning and bouffon in the UK and leads the Soho Theatre Comedy Lab Plus course. She trained at L'Ecole Philippe Gaulier.

Nicholas Armfield
Nick

Nicholas Trained at Guildhall School of Music and Drama. Theatre includes: *Richard III* (RSC); *Imperium Parts I and II* (Stratford/West End); *Pilgrims* (The Orange Tree Theatre); *A Rabbit Climbed a Ladder to the Moon* (The Place); *Artist Descending a Staircase* (King's Head). Television includes: Doctors (BBC). Film includes: Phaedra. Radio includes: *Camberwell Green*, *Dedication*, *The Story of the Lost Child*, *Those Who Leave and Those Who Stay*, *In Search of Lost Time* (BBC 4); *Sense and Sensibility* (Audible).

Lisa Carroll
Writer

Lisa is an Irish playwright based in the UK. Lisa trained on the Foundation Course at RADA and graduated from University College Dublin in 2012 with a B.A in English. She has undertaken writing programmes at the Lyric Hammersmith, the Royal Court and Headlong.

Previous work includes: *Three Cities* (Edinburgh Fringe), *Snapdragon* (Abbey Theatre) and *Cuckoo* (Soho Theatre, shortlisted for the Papatango Prize and Verity Bargate Award).

She is currently under commission to Ireland's National Theatre, the Abbey Theatre, writing a new play. In the summer of 2022, she was Writer on Attachment at the National Theatre. Also in 2022, she was Writer on Attachment at the Royal Shakespeare Company.

Bethany Pitts
Director

Bethany Pitts is an award winning director and dramaturg. Directing credits include: *The Beach House* by Jo Harper (Park Theatre); *Sirens* by Kenny Emson (Mercury Theatre); *Juniper and Jules* by Stephanie Martin (Soho Theatre/VAULT Festival – Show of the Week Award); the European premiere of Off-West End nominated Halley Feiffer's *A Funny Thing Happened on the Way to the Gynecologic Oncology Unit* (Finborough Theatre); *Fuck You Pay Me* by Joana Nastari (Bunker Theatre, VAULT/Edinburgh Festivals, People's Choice Award); *Brutal Cessation* by Milly Thomas (Assembly Edinburgh); *Spine* (Underbelly Edinburgh/Soho Theatre/UK tour – Fringe First Winner 2014); *Tether* by Isley Lynn (Underbelly Edinburgh); *FreeFall* (Pleasance Islington – Nominated for Off-West End Best Director).

Assistant/Associate directing includes: *Song at Twilight* by Noel Coward (Theatre Royal, Bath); *Abi* by Athia Sen Gupta (Derby Theatre/Queen's Theatre Hornchurch); *Frogman* by curious directive (Shoreditch Town Hall/Norwich Theatre Royal/UK tour) *Dark Vanilla Jungle* by Philip Ridley (Soho/Pleasance – Fringe First winner 2013); *Theatre Uncut* (Traverse Theatre – Fringe First Winner 2012/Young Vic 2013).

George Warren
Executive Producer, *Metal Rabbit*

George is Executive Producer at Rifco Theare. He worked as a script developer for Scottish Screen, Summit Entertainment (now Lionsgate), and Sky Drama, before literally running away to join the circus and producing for worldwide sensation Gandini Juggling from 2015–2018, with whom he won a Total Theatre Award. His subsequent career has included work with puppet musical-makers Monstro Theatre, new-writing specialists Metal Rabbit, with whom he wom two Broadway World Awards and sonic theatre company ERRATICA, for whom he also produces the podcast Soundwolds (winner of the 2023 BBC Audio

Award for Best Sound). He has toured productions across the USA, Europe, Australia and Asia and holds a diploma in script development from the National Film and TV School.

Cara Evans
Set and Costume Designer

Cara is a performance designer, an associate director at OPIA Collective and a reader at the Royal Court.

Theatre as Designer or Co-Designer includes: *The Living Newspaper* (Royal Court); *Sleepova* (Bush Theatre); *Sirens* (Mercury Colchester Studio); *Get Dressed!* (Unicorn Theatre); *Queer Upstairs* (Royal Court); *SK Shlomo: Breathe* (Royal Albert Hall); *Bright Half Life* (King's Head Theatre); *It's a Motherf**king Pleasure* (Soho and tour); *F**king Men* (Waterloo East); *The Beach House* (Park 90); *Blanket Ban* (New Diorama/Underbelly); *Ordinary Miracle* (NYT); *Instructions for a Teenage Armageddon* (Southwark Playhouse); *The Woman Who Turned into a Tree/ Refuge* (New Nordics Festival/Jackson's Lane). As Associate Designer for Chloe Lamford: *Teenage Dick* (Donmar School's Tour)

Louise Kempton
Intimacy Director

Louise Kempton is a movement director and intimacy director/ coordinator for theatre, TV and film. She trained in acting at Rose Bruford College, graduating in 2005, and later trained in Movement at Guildhall school. She was among the first cohort of intimacy coordinators under the mentorship of Ita O'Brien, Intimacy on Set, and has trained and worked extensively in this field since 2019. For television her Intimacy Coordinator credits include: *The Palace* (HBO); *Fifteen Love* (Amazon); *Smothered* (Sky); *Bad Sisters* (Apple TV); *Dangerous Liaisons* (Starz); *Chloe* (Amazon); *Masters of the Air* (Apple TV); *Gangs of London* (Sky) and *Young Wallander* (Netflix). For theatre her Intimacy Director credits include: *The Beach House* (Park Theatre); *Sirens* (Mercury Theatre); *Bangers* (Cardboard Citizens/Soho Theatre); *Intimate Apparel* and *Road* (Guildhall School); *An Adventure* (Bolton Octagon). Louise is a regular movement practitioner at various drama conservatoires including RADA, Royal Welsh College, Rose Bruford, Bristol Old Vic, Guildhall School and Mountview. She is a member of the BECTU intimacy branch.

Maja Lach
Stage Manager

Maja Lach is a freelance stage manager and migrant, based in London. Originally from Poland, she had never lived this close to the sea before and has been consistently cold since 2018. She's interested in creating accessible theatre with a focus on disability, community and immigrant issues. She wants to amplify queer, migrant and minority voices in theatre, starting with her own.

Her credits include: *Animate It! Live* for P&O Cruises, *Mudlarking* (Bush Theatre); *Circ-ulate* (Jacksons Lane); *Addictive Beat* (Boundless Theatre) and *Diary of a Somebody* (Seven Dials Playhouse). She is currently working as Show Operations Controller and Duty Manager at *Tomb Raider: The LIVE Experience*, and preparing for a production of *Places I Never Think About* at the Lion & Unicorn Theatre.

Adam Maxey
Assistant Stage Manager

Adam is a classically trained opera singer from Dorset, and has multiple performance credits across theatre and opera in the UK and abroad. He is a graduate of both the Guildhall School of Music and Drama and the Royal College of Music.

Adam has worked with leading opera companies across the UK including Glyndebourne Festival and Touring Operas, English Touring Opera and Welsh National Opera. He has been involved in outreach and education productions with companies such as Nevill Holt Opera, ETO, Garsington Opera and Mahogany Opera.

Simon Paris
Associate Producer

Simon is an innovative theatre-maker who enjoys exploring the boundaries between audience and performer. His shows are bold, funny, and unapologetic in their skepticism towards authority. He often working with new writers, devising with ensembles, and putting a fresh spin on classic plays. His work is often compelling to young, daring audiences.

Currently, Simon serves as Artistic Director for Say It Again, Sorry?, an interactive theatre company, as well as Producer at Metal Rabbit Productions. His remarkable ability to craft unforgettable experiences on stage continues to inspire and captivate audiences across the UK.

Highlighted work includes: *The Importance of Being... Earnest?* (Edinburgh Fringe Festival, Pleasance, Beyond 2022); *The Prince* (Southwark Playhouse, The Large, 2022); *Evelyn* (Southwark Playhouse, The Large, 2022); *Monopoly Lifesized* (Selladoor, 2022); *Bring It On: The Musical* (Southbank Centre, 2022); *Not Our Play* (Rosemary Branch Theatre, 2022) and *News Revue* (2020).

Oli Seymour
Associate Producer

A theatre and audio producer, Oli's recent projects include *Stopping to Notice*, a series that captures the small but magical moments of everyday life in binaural sound, and Metal Rabbit's *Mediocre White Male* (Park Theatre, King's Head Theatre), which has received four and five-star reviews across the press.

He assisted on Metal Rabbit's *Spiderfly* (Theatre503, December 2019), and produced *Hear Myself Think*, a drama series aimed at helping listeners engage with their wellbeing, as well as *The People Outside*, a comedy drama set in a mysterious seaside town.

Peter Small
Lighting Designer

Peter is an Offie and Theatre & Technology Award nominated lighting designer working across theatre, dance and opera. In 2018, Peter was nominated for two Off West End Best Lighting Awards for *Black Mountain* and *A Girl in School Uniform* (*Walks in to a Bar*).

Theatre includes: *The Caucasian Chalk Circle*, *The Priory* and *A Skull in Connemara* (Dailes Theatre, Latvia); *Dido's Bar* (Dash Arts UK Tour); *Kathy and Stella Solve a Murder* (Summerhall, Edinburgh Fringe); *Twelfth Night* (Kew Gardens); *What Remains For Us* (Bristol Old Vic); *The Great Murder Mystery* and *The Great Christmas Feast* (The Lost Estate); *Red* (Polka Theatre); *2020: Collections* (Tara Arts); *Baby Reindeer* (Bush and Edinburgh Fringe); *Lady Chatterley's Lover* (UK tour); *Square Go*

(UK tour, 59E59 Theater New York and Edinburgh Fringe); *Lit* (Nottingham Playhouse tour and Online); *All Or Nothing* (West End and tour).

Dominic Brennan
Sound Designer

Dominic Brennan is a composer and sound designer from West London. Previous shows include: *STRIKE!* (Southwark Playhouse); *Mediocre White Male* (Park Theatre); *Spiderfly* (Theatre 503); *Cuckoo* (Soho Theatre); *We're Staying Right Here* (Park Theatre); *Shackleton and his Stowaway* (Park Theatre) and *The Universal Machine* (New Diorama Theatre). In 2017 he won the Off-West End Award for Sound Design for his work on *Down and Out in Paris and London* (New Diorama Theatre). Other work includes music for adverts, short films and a sound installation at the Princess of Wales Conservatory in Kew Gardens.

Martin Poile
Casting director

Martin is a freelance Casting Director. He is also Senior Casting Assistant at the Royal Shakespeare Company working across all in-house productions, workshops, readings and special events for the RSC.

As Casting Director: *Falkland Sound*, *The Empress*, *Cowbois* (RSC); *Twelfth Night* (RSC/UK tour); *Boundless as the Sea*, *Miss Littlewood* (RSC/Cunard QM2); *Felix and Fanny* (Barbican); *The Dwarfs* (White Bear); *SHTF* (Kandinsky, Schauspielhaus Wien, Vienna).

Recent credits as Casting Assistant include: *My Neighbour Totoro* (RSC/Barbican); *The Magician's Elephant*, *The Boy in the Dress* (RSC).

Acknowledgements

A heartfelt thanks to:

Everyone who has supported and cheerleaded this play from its inception, including George Warren, Oli Seymour, Simon Paris, Tamar Saphra, Tommo Fowler, Philip Shelley, Lekan Lawal, Gillian Greer, Chris Truscott, Stewart Pringle, Daniel Donnelly, Rían Smith, Jesse Weaver, Jonathan Kinnersley, Matt Applewhite and all at Nick Hern Books. Thanks also to Shawna Scott of Sex Siopa for incredibly helpful consultation.

The brilliant Beth Pitts, the delightful Elf Lyons and Nick Armfield, and our whole amazing team.

My friends and family, Aki and Dan, Alfie and Ian (but mainly Alfie).

THE MISANDRIST

Lisa Carroll

For George

Characters

RACHEL, *late twenties/early thirties*
NICK, *late twenties/early thirties*

This text went to press before the end of rehearsals and so may differ slightly from the play as performed.

Content Warning

This play discusses themes of sexual assault and suicide.

Notes on the Text

This play is for two actors (one female, one male) in their late twenties/early thirties. Each has a central character (Rachel and Nick) but also embodies other characters as indicated.

The play is set now, in London.

The stage space is transmutable and fluid: we travel to a number of different locations and times. As little faff as possible is ideal.

Punctuation and Stage Directions

A slash (/) indicates where one character begins speaking over another.

A dash (–) indicates that the character speaking is cut off by an interruption from another character, or a thought cutting across what they were saying.

Ellipses (…) suggest space for thought in the line.

A space within a character's lines suggests a pause, hesitation, thought, and/or change in tactics. These need to be acknowledged in performance.

Text appearing in [square brackets] is unspoken.

A (*Beat.*) is shorter than a (*Pause.*) which is shorter than a (*Silence.*).

PART ONE

Terrifying Christmas Cheer

December. An office Christmas party. RACHEL *wears a Santa hat.*

RACHEL *addresses us directly:*

RACHEL. I'm planning on stealing my colleague's Tupperware. I know it's Christmas – it's our work Christmas party – but I MUST have it. In fact lately I *can't stop*, I mean *literally cannot stop* thinking about Tupperware.

Tupperware, good Tupperware: the kind that doesn't leak, doesn't warp in the dishwasher, doesn't get stained or smell... the Sistema stuff, basically, like this one: it's the *gold standard* of food containers. There's truly nothing better. I dream about it sometimes.

The boxes fit into each other! They just stack so perfectly. You know what, there's structure, that's what it is. No surprises. Absolutely no bullshit with these: what you see is what you get.

Anyway, look, I've never stolen Tupperware before, because I, of all people, know just how precious it can be, but Monika, who owns this one, absolutely deserves it for this single reason: she calls herself The Office Christmas Elf.

She organised this horrendous Christmas party, and she's been wearing light-up Christmas jumpers *and* tinsel *every day* for the last month. Possibly longer, not sure, I only started in November.

I'm contracting for a Cultural Relations organisation. Huge, thousands of staff around the world. Totally male, pale and stale at the top, of course, but not to worry – it has a robust Equality, Diversity and Inclusion policy which it constantly says it's *trying* to stick to.

But – Monika – I mean, think we can agree that that is a *terrifying* level of Christmas cheer. She's a walking fire-hazard. A caricature. I know I'm risking the possibility of a proper permanent contract here for short term gain, but she simply *does not deserve* this Tupperware, whereas it'll make *me* feel *really good*. She probably doesn't even know my fucking name, anyway, no one else here does.

Shady as hell, she goes to swoop on the Tupperware, scans the room, then freezes when she spots NICK:

There's a... Creepy little man staring at me. While I stare at this Tupperware.

Hold... Hold... GO!

She snatches the Tupperware. Looks over at NICK *who definitely noticed.*

Bollocks!

Meet-Cute (Gross)

An All Bar One in Central.

RACHEL. You've been staring at me all night, / I saw you staring at me earlier –

NICK. Have I? Sorry just – you're SO tall

RACHEL. Wow. Is your mind as small as your body?

NICK. Never said it was a bad thing

RACHEL. Um, neither did I!?

NICK. Not that many women are tall... Amazonian!

RACHEL. Amazonian... As in... I could crush a whole, entire man between my thighs?

NICK. Uh... Yeah. Again, not necessarily a bad thing –

RACHEL. Again, didn't say it was.

Look, Monika's starting a conga line. You look like you'd be into that kind of thing, so...

NICK. Are you... friends with that lady?

RACHEL. NO, no, *no*. I'd like, stab her if I could.

NICK. Wow.

No, she does need stabbing, you're right

RACHEL. I know! Okay, I'm gonna tell you something

NICK. Okay

RACHEL. I stole her Tupperware

NICK. That was *her* Tupperware?

RACHEL. Yep. I just needed to... really hit her where it hurts.

NICK. *Nice*

RACHEL. Yeah?

NICK. Yeah

Beat.

And you're –

RACHEL. Now the proud owner of a high quality piece of / Tupperware –

NICK. No, sorry, I mean *great,* but you're –

RACHEL. A... Virgo moon rising?

NICK. Your name?

RACHEL. OH – Rachel

NICK. Nick

Beat.

RACHEL. Cool well, great to meet you Nick, and um, thank you for calling me a Giant Lady –

NICK. I didn't call you a – no it's – it's attractive – your height –

RACHEL. Cool. I'm gonna go home. I've got this risotto in the fridge I'm gonna heat up, I'm pretty excited about it.

NICK. Outdone by congealed rice, *okay*

RACHEL. Sorry?

NICK. Look, can I get you a drink?

RACHEL. But… my rice

NICK. Let me try this again – Rachel – it's great to meet you – I'm currently trying to hit on you – it's going terribly

RACHEL. Yeah no I know

NICK. So… can I get you a drink?

Fuck Him

RACHEL *and her boss, Fiona (Northern Irish, late-thirties) are smoking outside.*

NICK *plays Fiona throughout the play.*

NICK. Fuck him.

RACHEL. I barely –

NICK. You need to fuck him. Do it.

To us:

RACHEL. My line manager, Fiona, is in her late-thirties, married, and I've noticed she's like, one hundred per cent a functioning alcoholic? I think that whole famine, Troubles, Catholic church, eight-hundred-years-of-English-rule trauma is definitely in there trying to work its way out. It's very dark.

We both feel weird about working for this 'soft power' organisation, since Britain colonised our ancestors, and now we're helping it culturally colonise the world, but we also both really like that the hours are flexible and you can work from home?

To Fiona:

Fiona, I feel like HR would have a *fit* if they knew you'd –

NICK. I don't give a shit, you need to put on the Big Girl Pants and go bang that man.

RACHEL. We work for the same –

NICK. Doesn't matter – listen, how often does a person come up to you in real life any more?

RACHEL. I don't know if that justifies –

NICK. Let's be real, you *desperately* need to catch a dick

RACHEL. How do you know?

NICK. *Bang* of desperation off you, I mean when did you last have sex?

RACHEL. Jesus

NICK. When did you last have sex?

RACHEL. Last week

NICK. *When did you last have sex?*

RACHEL.…Two years ago.

NICK. Jesus wept

RACHEL. It's for *good* reason

NICK. Babe, it's time to get back on the fucking horse

RACHEL. I've got this risotto at home that I / really wanna –

NICK. Oh you are *such* a fucking square, go fuck him or I won't extend your contract

RACHEL. What? You can't –

NICK. JUST GO!

Pink Margs O'Clock

Back in the bar.

RACHEL. That's for you –

NICK. That? What is it?

RACHEL. Pink margarita – they had an offer so I –

NICK. I can't – I can't drink that

RACHEL. Go on! Cut loose!

NICK. I mean this is gonna sound bad, but like…

RACHEL. Looks girly?

NICK. Yeah, if I'm honest

RACHEL. But it's delicious

NICK. Yeah I'm sure it is

RACHEL. So, what… is sugar gay now?

NICK. NO no, no. I'm not saying that, it –

That is delicious actually

RACHEL. And you were gonna deny yourself.

NICK. But I can't drink it

RACHEL. Okay, more for me, sláinte

NICK. Shame you don't have an Irish accent

RACHEL. I know, the only time I can do it is when I'm imitating my mum

NICK. Go on

RACHEL. So for context, Irish mammies don't do sex education – so this was the birds and the bees talk I got.

I'm about thirteen, we're like, walking to school or something, and out of nowhere she just stops, looks me dead in the eye and goes:

'Rachel, don't you ever, *ever* have sex until you're married!'

NICK. Terrifying. Bit arousing.

RACHEL. And obviously... I've done as I was told

NICK. Obviously

RACHEL. Obviously.

Sorry – do you know that guy? Over there, like, watching us –

NICK. Huh? Oh, yeah, that's my flatmate – Eddie

RACHEL. Oh... is this a – did he put you up to this?

NICK. Put me up to what?

RACHEL. I dunno, insult the tall lady, hit on me as a joke or –

NICK. No! No no not at all, no, not a joke

RACHEL. Why's he here?

NICK. Oh he doesn't have... that many friends... so I told him to come by

RACHEL. Oh. That's kind of... weird and sweet. Also, a shame, cos you're about to ditch him. Uber's outside.

NICK. What – to...?

RACHEL. My house

NICK. Wow you're *really* passionate about that risotto

RACHEL. No, for both of us

NICK. Oh! Wow, alright Speedy Gonzales

RACHEL. We need to move quickly before I think about this too much

NICK. See: taking control, Amazonian

RACHEL. You keep – do you have a crushing fantasy or something?

NICK. NO – no, no, nooooo. I mean, unless you – no. Nope. I just enjoy plain, straightforward, I would even say, perfunctory sex. No frills. No expression, even. Just. Yeah.

RACHEL.…You are a strange little man.

NICK. I know. Not little, just saying – but yes.

RACHEL. Do you want a slice of this cake or not?

Vibe Killer

They sit awkwardly, silently in the Uber.

RACHEL. We give Eddie a lift.

NICK. I mean, you gotta save the pennies, in this economy

RACHEL. He sits in the middle.

NICK. Eddie is an A1 guy – developer – speaks better code than he does English.

RACHEL. Doesn't speak to me, ask my name even, or laugh at my jokes

NICK. I'm trying to teach him, you know, a bit of *game*.

RACHEL. He's eating a slighly congealed katsu curry from Wasabi and it *stinks* –

   NICK *plays Eddie – sweet and derpy:*

NICK. Want a taste?

   As NICK *and* RACHEL *again*.

RACHEL. He doesn't even ask you, he just holds the spoon to your lips

NICK. He doesn't, I'm not a baby

   To us:

   We drop him off, he's gone.

   To each other:

   Great guy.

RACHEL. Seems it!

Now they're suddenly alone(ish) for the first time.

 Nearly there!

NICK *tries to, cool as a cucumber, slip his arm around* RACHEL.

You know that face *all* guys make when they lunge in to kiss you?

They both make the face, to us.

Also attempting to deal with the bumpy road, car braking, speed bumps, etc., they eventually kiss. But mid-kiss, arrive at their destination.

OMG Actual Sex

RACHEL*'s flat. Just after.*

NICK. Nice flat

RACHEL. Ah it's a bit… Live-laugh-love, isn't it? My housemate has *zero* taste. Her parents bought it for her. Making her an extremely youthful landlord.

NICK. Mate of yours, or?

RACHEL. Oh, no, no, SpareRoom. She's out, by the way – she's got this, like, boring little boyfriend. At his, most of the time.

NICK. Cool

RACHEL. Just gonna put this baby away.

RACHEL *holds the Tupperware like a rare jewel.*

Her phone rings – she looks at the caller ID and rejects it.

NICK. You can take that if you –

RACHEL. No no it's fine, just my dad, hah, *baaaad* timing

NICK. Whenever I get an actually phonecall from a relative at a weird time I'm always immediately like OKAY THAT'S IT, SOMEONE'S DEAD

(*Re. the Tupperware cupboard.*) That's an impressive Tupperware stacking system

RACHEL. Thank you so much, I dedicated hours to that

Pause.

NICK. That your room, yeah?

RACHEL. Do you want a drink? I've got gin / if you –

NICK. I'm alright –

RACHEL. Think I have some crisps somewhere if you / want a sn–

NICK. Nah I'm alright, honestly

RACHEL. ...Risotto? Microwaved risotto? Very tasty.

NICK. Rachel, if you... want me to go, / I can...

RACHEL. No no no no no no no I just – I just realised I, like, *really* don't know you, like at all

NICK. We don't have to do anything / you don't –

RACHEL. Are you crazy? My vagina's almost hermetically sealed at this point – just... Also please don't murder me

NICK. *What?*

RACHEL. No murdering

NICK. But I've been really looking forward to [murdering you]

RACHEL. No no no don't joke, no jokes, just, supress your murderous impulses

NICK. Where's this come from? Have I got vibes?

RACHEL. No, just... You're a man. And... men murder women all the time

NICK. I've managed to avoid it –

RACHEL. Okay cool, great, I'm just – I'm just pre-emptively
saying, I would not like to be murdered. That includes
choking me to death and saying I wanted it cos I'm telling
you now, for the record, I do not consent to death. Or anal.
For the time being.

NICK. Okay. Understood. I promise I will not kill you. Or put it
in your butt.

RACHEL. Okay... Do you do this a lot?

NICK. No, I told you, I don't murder –

RACHEL. No, no, just... Go home with women you've just
met?

NICK. Errr... I mean if you're asking if I'm like, dating, seeing
people... Odd one night stand here and there... Then yeah?

Here, look at me?

They look at each other.

It's okay. Okay?

RACHEL. Okay.

They get close. They're nose to nose, about to kiss. NICK
giggles.

What?!

NICK. Sorry, sorry, nothing –

Giggles again

Sorry – I'm so sorry, I've just never like... Looked *up* into
someone's eyes before

RACHEL. Oh my Gooooood

NICK. This is my first time with a tall lady

RACHEL. Stoooooop

NICK. I'm excited

RACHEL. So *sillyyyyy* stoooopppppp

　Also, we need to use a condom.

NICK. Okay now that's one step / too far

RACHEL. You're not serious

NICK. Can you at least take the Santa hat off?

RACHEL.…No.

She turns the lights off.

Time for SEX!

The rule is: No bad sex miming, no dry humping. Maybe it's an interpretive dance. Maybe it's battling with toy lightsabers. Who knows.

NICK. Ooooh, that's – can you? YEAH

RACHEL. Bit lower – yep – yep – YESSSSSSS

BOTH. YES!

Etc. They both come.

Maybe afterwards they both light a cigarette or some other silly cliché.

RACHEL. Are you going!?

NICK. Yeah… gotta be up at, like, six tomorrow

RACHEL. So get some sleep here?

NICK. Nah, prefer my own bed – do you wanna put your number in my phone?

RACHEL. Hold on, where's the…

NICK. What?

RACHEL. Where's the condom?

NICK. Uh… Should be… I dunno

RACHEL. Where the fuck – you wore a condom right?

NICK. Yeah, yeah course –

RACHEL. Did you?! *Shit –*

NICK. Yeah I swear cos like, I'm actually sort of allergic to latex so my dick is, sort of currently on fire, but I was also like, very distracted by… having excellent sex, so

RACHEL. Where –

They search the room.

NICK. Not in the bin, no?

RACHEL. No

Fuck, where would it – ?

Same thought at the same time.

Fuck – fuck is it – ?

NICK. Is it…?

They look at each other. RACHEL's on the verge of tears now, pure panic.

RACHEL. Oh my God do you think it's… / Oh my God

NICK. Has that happened before? / Can that happen?

RACHEL. What if it is… Still in there, oh my God should we call 999? / What if I get like some kind of toxic shock syndrome, should we –

NICK. Okay okay okay okay I'm sure it's fine, calm calm calm calm calm let's think, let's –

They look at each other again, realising what's going to have to be done.

RACHEL. I don't know if I can ever look you in the eye again if –

NICK. I think we have to

They let it sink in.

Star Trek: Enterprise *music or something similar. He has to conduct the search.*

Somehow we enter the world of RACHEL*'s womb. They are both mortified, but* NICK *is very sweet about it.*

To us:

It wasn't in there.

RACHEL. It wasn't fucking in there.

Back in scene:

NICK. Then where the...

They go back to room searching.

RACHEL *turns around and the condom is stuck to her back*

Oh my God don't move!

RACHEL. What!?

NICK. Don't move!

He peels it off her back and holds it up triumphantly.

RACHEL. NOOOOOOO

NICK. YEAHHHHHH

RACHEL. Fuuuuucking hell! Fucking hell!

Some kind of celebratory, crusty condom-swinging dance of joy and relief.

They both flop down on the bed, relieved, mortified, laughing, maybe quietly weeping.

Oh my God

NICK. Oh my God

RACHEL. Oh MY God...

I've died. I'm dead inside.

So silly

NICK. *So* silly. Fuck. What a rollercoaster.

Okay. I'm gonna be a zombie tomorrow

RACHEL. Yeah, yeah, no worries

NICK. Okay

> RACHEL, *now the shock, horror and relief have passed, sits curled up in utter humiliation at what's just occurred. She quietly weeps.*

> NICK, *just on his way out, notices. Hesitates. Then puts his stuff down.*

Okay, scoot

RACHEL. I'm fine, these are tears of laughter, I'm fine –

NICK. Scoot, come on, I'm breaking the first commandment here, give me some credit

RACHEL. First / commandment?

NICK. *Never* stay over. Scoot.

> NICK *shoves/scoots her over, turns her on her side, and spoons her.*

I'm like a little jetpack!

RACHEL. Fuck! *So* silly

> RACHEL *laugh-cries more.* NICK *folds her back over and folds his arm around her.*

Morning Sleepy Head

Next morning. NICK *creeps out of bed, quietly pulls his clothes on.* RACHEL *wakes up and he starts.*

RACHEL. Sleep alright?

NICK. Uh yeah – sorry I – fuck, I'm late –

RACHEL. Do you want a shower?

NICK. No – I've gotta – sorry – I'll text you?

RACHEL. Wait, hold on, hold on – can I just check –

We're… in a committed relationship now, right?

NICK. Huh? Oh, yeah, ha, I was uh – gonna propose later – at work

RACHEL. Brill, can't wait

Nick. You don't need to flee. I'm not gonna eat you alive.

NICK....Sorry. Okay. This was actually very fun

RACHEL. It was a real treat to not have to fake an orgasm. I think we should do this again

NICK. I, um

RACHEL. What? That breaks the second commandment?

NICK. Uh... Kind of, yeah

What if we... stick to the first commandment? No staying over, NO spooning. Just... delightful... sex?

Milk Alternatives

NICK, *as Fiona, that morning, smoking area in front of the office entrance.*

NICK. Did you fuck him?

RACHEL. Morning, Fiona. HOW ARE YOU?

NICK. Did you fuck him?

RACHEL. Gimme one of those –

NICK. You better've fucked him

RACHEL. I fucked him. Happy?

NICK. More relieved than anything

By the way, did you hear, see or read what happened to Monika's Tupperware last night? She's been storming round the place saying someone's nicked it – like, *get a life*, it's just Tupperware

RACHEL. Exactly, get a life, get a *massive* life.

So. I did it. Are you extending my contract?

NICK. Oh, I never had that kind of power

RACHEL. You *what?*

NICK. Do you want a coffee? I'm on a whole journey into the world of alternative milks at the moment – oat, almond, soya. I feel like it's my character arc.

RACHEL. I'm alright

NICK. So. You gonna fuck him again? One shag's not gonna cure whatever you've got

To us:

RACHEL. I am. I am gonna fuck him again.

Bangathon

Later. RACHEL *and* NICK *are going at it.*

RACHEL. Monika… is apparently… raging around the office… saying someone… stole… her Tupperware…

NICK. Oh God, oh God, I hope she's furious

RACHEL. She's livid

NICK. Uh

RACHEL. The more livid she is the better I feel

NICK. Oh God… And she has no idea, she has no idea you took it?

RACHEL. None

NICK. Uh

RACHEL. She'll never know

NICK. I'm gonna come, oh God

They both finish.

Playful, the two of them tell us:

RACHEL. Got some latex-free condoms

NICK. So sweet! We fuck on my sofa

RACHEL. We do it on the bathroom floor

NICK. We do it on my single bed underneath my hanging collage of Pokémon cards

RACHEL. Eddie's knocks on the door – 'Can you keep it down?'

NICK. Mate, I *told* you to wear your noise-cancelling headphones!

RACHEL. What if we skip work to fuck?

NICK. We skip work to fuck. I'm not afraid to stick it to the man!

RACHEL. What if we… fuck *at* work?

NICK. I'm no pussy – we fuck in the third-floor toilets.

RACHEL. We fuck in a park

NICK. We fuck in a Pret

RACHEL. We fuck at SoulCycle

NICK. We fuck in M&M's world. What if we…

RACHEL. Yeah!?

NICK. Do it without a condom this time?

RACHEL. Oh. No. We fuck on my housemate's bed, mainly cos I know she'd HATE IT

NICK. We fuck on the top floor of a bus

RACHEL. We film ourselves fucking then we fuck while we watch ourselves fuck

BOTH. META

RACHEL's *phone rings* –

NICK. That your phone?

RACHEL. Ignore it

NICK. I can't... It's throwing off my rhythm

RACHEL. It's just my dad

NICK. At 2 a.m.?

RACHEL. We fuck every which way –

NICK. Reverse cowgirl, inverse cowgirl, cat-cow, classic cowgirl, converse cowgirl

I *do* think this would be better without a condom –

RACHEL. NO. We need to fuck on my boss's desk

NICK. Really?

RACHEL. Honestly, she'd be so proud.

NICK. Sit on my face, sit on my face –

RACHEL. Wh-what if I crush you?!

NICK. YES, SIT ON MY FACE

Would you *consider* –

RACHEL. I told you, I'm not not wearing a condom

NICK. Why not? Most girls are on the pill, aren't they?

RACHEL. Are you still sleeping with all these other girls?

NICK....

RACHEL. l don't *really* wanna go on the – okay – we can fuck without a condom if I'm the only person you're fucking, I don't want an STI

NICK. Okay

RACHEL. Really?

NICK. Yeah

RACHEL. *Bollocks*

NICK. We swab

RACHEL. We send them off

NICK. We wait

BOTH. We fuck in a public toilet to celebrate a clean bill of health

RACHEL. We fuck without a condom and he loses his damn mind

Pull my hair, pull my –

NICK. Really? –

RACHEL. ARE YOU A MAN OR A MOUSE?

NICK. Can you, like, choke me? Really choke me? Like test the limits of my mortality choke me?

RACHEL. Yeah go on then. Can I have a go?

NICK. Course.

RACHEL. Do you fancy –

NICK. I was gonna ask [the same thing]

RACHEL. Light spank?

NICK. Please!

RACHEL. We fuck like it's going out of style

NICK. I fuck her all the way into next year – can I tie you up?

RACHEL. You first. What, scared?

NICK. No. Nope. Not scared of anything.

RACHEL. What's your surname by the way?

NICK. What? Marsden. You?

RACHEL. Mulligan. We do a lifetime's worth of fucking

NICK. If anything, it's almost too much fucking

RACHEL. I've bankrupted myself with sex toys and I'm pretty much permanently walking like John Wayne

NICK. My back hurts, I'm flagging

RACHEL. And I'm running out of ideas

Breather.

And then…

NICK. I don't know what comes over me…

RACHEL. It just happens

NICK. In the throes of passion

RACHEL. He's moves my finger towards

NICK. It's like a magnetic pull, a calling

RACHEL. He's definitely… moving my finger –

NICK. Towards the / bum

RACHEL. Up his bum

NICK. JESUS MARY AND JOSEPH

Both stunned at NICK*'s explosive orgasm.*

My Moral Compass is Intact, Thank You

Day. RACHEL *and Fiona smoke.*

NICK. Peg him

RACHEL. *What* him?

NICK. Peg him!

Get yersel a strap-on, bend him over and bang him up the arse

RACHEL. Holy shit Fiona – have you done this?!

NICK. Oh I'd kill to peg a man. Bastard husband won't entertain it.

RACHEL. I really don't know if this is me

NICK. Fine, get bored of each other then.

Here, I've not told anybody this, but I've been having an affair

RACHEL. What? Who? Who with?

NICK. Simon. Found him on Hinge.

RACHEL. What!?

NICK. That's what boredom does to you. I do feel a bit bad about it but like, honestly I'm not built for monogamy? It's such, like, *bullshit* that society says –

RACHEL. Then why did you get married?

NICK. I dunno… everyone I know was getting married, everyone was telling us to get married cos we were together donkey's years

RACHEL. Are you… gonna tell him?

NICK. Eh… nah.

RACHEL. Have you ever been cheated on?

NICK. Pffff, no. Not *that* stupid

RACHEL. It's the worst fucking feeling you can ever imagine.

NICK. Oh shit

RACHEL. Yeah.

NICK. *Oh shiiiiit*

RACHEL. Yeah. You're not gonna stop, are you?

NICK. No. I know what'll make you feel better –

RACHEL. Peg / that man

NICK. Peg that little man, aye

More Dildos Than You Could Ever Dream

To us:

RACHEL. You turn up a nondescript alleyway, a stone's throw from Old Street station. A bell tinkles as you step in the door. Everything is a rich pink and the furnishings are plush. It's like stepping into a giant, welcoming vagina. You're greeted by a friendly, leather clad attendant, with bright red hair, a severe fringe and large rimmed glasses.

NICK *plays the attendant, Jenny.*

NICK. Here for the workshop, my darling?

RACHEL. Uh, yeah

NICK. Great! I'm Jenny. We're starting in five through there, so for now just grab yourself a glass of prosecco and a cupcake and take a seat!

To us:

RACHEL. Sexually imposing Jenny pulls back a deep red velvet curtain, and I enter a room decked with / dildos.

NICK. Dildos.

Dildos –

RACHEL. On the walls

NICK. Dildos –

RACHEL. On the shelves

NICK. Dildos –

RACHEL. Standing proudly on on each of the small tables arranged in a semicircle.

NICK. Dildos –

RACHEL. Of every shape and size

NICK. More dildos than you ever knew possible

RACHEL. There's a wealthy Lithuanian woman with lip-filler-lips, bright blonde hair and wearing all black shiny lamé. A couple of Spanish girls who look uncannily alike. And a woman in a flannel shirt and a lady I'm guessing is her partner. I sit next to a nervous heterosexual couple – he's short, bearded, red-faced. She looks like a primary school teacher.

NICK. Okay folks! Thanks for coming! I'm your gracious host and we're all friends here tonight, so no need to feel shy or embarrassed! We run classes like this all the time, and we're all about empowering you and making sure you're having sex that's safe, consensual, and most importantly – FUN!

RACHEL *plays Hannah, the other workshop leader –*

RACHEL. Okay, so I'm Hannah! I've been working here about a year trust me when I say, I've really heard it all, it is *impossible* to shock me!

First things first, we're all going to go round and introduce ourselves, and I want you to tell us: what your imaginary penis is called! Okay?

I'll start, I'm Hannah, I work here, and my imaginary penis is called… Montgomery.

NICK *plays the participants:*

NICK. Hi I'm Justina, I'm from Lithuania, been living here four years now. I have a lover – he is twenty-two and he wants me to dominate him, so I came.

RACHEL. Great! And your penis name?

NICK. I don't know

RACHEL. Anything at all?

NICK. All I can think of right now is my father's name

RACHEL. Okay! Let's move on –

NICK, *as Jenny, points to* RACHEL.

NICK. You there, penis name?

RACHEL. It's bad enough I'm even here, let alone – BRUCE

NICK. Bruce!!! Why Bruce?

RACHEL. I dunno just sounds like a Big Dick Name

NICK. Okay! And what brought you here Rachel?

To us:

RACHEL. I can't stop thinking about it. Literally cannot stop. It's like Tupperware has lost all meaning and all I picture when I'm going to sleep at night is strap-ons. I'm gonna help this man discover his prostate – discover himself even, who knows. But mainly – MAINLY – I wanna do this because I'm an extremely exciting, adventurous, GENEROUS lover, that's why, that's mainly why

To Jenny:

My boss told me to do it?

NICK. Well she sounds fun!

RACHEL. I hate her – no I – yeah, I think I hate her

As Jenny and Hannah:

NICK. OKAY! LET'S GET INTO IT FOLKS! So the first thing we're going to look at tonight is…

RACHEL. Anatomy!!!!!

She gets out a huge diagram of the male genitalia.

NICK. So, obviously, that is the penis

RACHEL. And what's this?

NICK. The balls!

RACHEL. And up here we have?

NICK. The prostate! Okay – so how many of you have done a cheeky finger up the bum during sex?

RACHEL slowly raises her hand.

Good work, Rachel!

RACHEL *is thrilled with herself.*

Right folks! Let's talk equipment…

RACHEL. First thing you're gonna need –

To us:

NICK. Dildos, butt plugs… Big, small, marbled, jewel encrusted… We've got anything you like.

A wall of dildos. RACHEL *stands before it in awe.* RACHEL *reverently takes down an unbelievably enormous dildo.*

RACHEL. But my eye is caught: the Mistress Twister

She's as big as my arm. She shouldn't even be real –

NICK. Oop – that's not for beginners, darling! Try this one –

Jenny hands RACHEL *a more reasonable dildo.*

Let me help you pop that on. Well! Look at you!

RACHEL *struts up to the mirror – fuck – she's actually caught off guard by it – shit – she looks GOOD.*

Wearing the strap-on, she feels her posture adjust – she's standing taller, hands on hips, big dick swinging. She has discovered… big dick energy.

She admires herself from every angle.

There's no going back now.

Whose Butt Is It Anyway?

A few days later, NICK*'s flat.*

RACHEL. I got something, little treat

NICK. Oh yeah? Like… a sexy treat?

RACHEL *unveils a buttplug. They both stand in awe.*

It shines, like a beacon of hope.

So you want to...

RACHEL. Yeah! Do... you?

NICK. Yeah!

RACHEL. You know what it is?

NICK. Oh yeah

RACHEL. Amazing – I wasn't sure if you'd be into –

NICK. Oh yeah, yeah, for sure

RACHEL. Okay great – I'm glad you're, like, so open

NICK. Yeah, yeah. Like I think part of it is like it's... a bit transgressive?

RACHEL. Sure

NICK. Like my dad would be absolutely appalled

RACHEL. Love that we're bringing him into the bedroom

NICK. Ha. And I guess, like, less people go in there

RACHEL. Sorry?

NICK. Like, you know for girls, like, less people go... round the back... so it's a bit more... like? Special?

RACHEL. OH you think it's... for me?

NICK. Yeah! Yeah I mean it's not for me, is it?

RACHEL. Um...

NICK. What?

RACHEL. What?

NICK. What?

RACHEL. ...What?

NICK. What?

RACHEL. Did you also just describe my arsehole as like... an exclusive club? Like a VIP club? Cos I'll let just anyone into my vagina?

NICK....No. No I did not, hold on hold on hold on, do YOU wanna do me... in the... in the... in the... backside?

RACHEL. Would you like me to? I feel like maybe you'd like me to?

Beat. NICK *ROARS laughing.* RACHEL *watches wide-eyed.*

He pauses. He kind of expected her to join in the laughter – she usually does. Beat.

Aaaahahahaa / haaaaahhahahahaaaa

Phew. He joins in. They pass the buttplug back and forth during the following:

NICK. Aaaahahahahaaaaaaaaaaa – WOW you – you really got me

RACHEL. Got you!

NICK. REALLY got me

RACHEL. Haaaaa, I thought you wanted me to –

NICK. You were gonna –

RACHEL. Imagine! Me pegging you!

NICK. Oh my God is that what it's – pegging!? Aaaaahahahahaha, pegging

RACHEL. Baahahahahaaa – me all – me all dressed up, dominatrix style, strap-on / – ahahahha imagine ME –

NICK. Baaaaaaaaaa you'd love that wouldn't / you?

RACHEL. YOU'd love that who are / YOU kidding?

NICK. Crazy, crazy man, you – you you – to me? Nah, nah, no, NO

RACHEL. NOT into that

NICK. NOT INTO THAT, DEFINITELY NOT INTO THAT

RACHEL. Nope

NICK. Nope!

RACHEL. Nope

The laughter dies.

Then RACHEL *start giggling again – it's infectious.*

You know what was funny?

NICK. What?

But she's laughing too much.

What?!!

RACHEL. No just, remember that time, that time – sorry

NICK. What!!! What time!?

RACHEL. That time I stuck my finger up your butt and made you come like a train?

Beat. NICK *goes to hand the buttplug back to her.*

Why don't you just... hold onto it for a while?

Beggin' for a Peggin'

Could be fun if a lot of this discussion happens during sex.

RACHEL. I bring pegging up every chance I get.

NICK. Before sex, during sex, after sex

RACHEL. I've got peg on the brain and I won't rest until he has too

NICK. Is it sexist if I say... She *nags* me?

RACHEL. You know what'll help you *not* be sexist? Letting me peg you

NICK. Rachel, I can be a feminist without a dildo in my ass

RACHEL. You know what'd make you an even better feminist?

NICK. Stop it

To us:

RACHEL. I should also mention actually, my contract finishing.

NICK. Oh?

RACHEL. Yeah, I no longer design outstanding content experiences for the cultural relations organisation

NICK. Uh... I should mention... I managed to get a fixed term contract in the bag.

RACHEL. Really...? Nice! Hah, no more fucking at work

NICK. No

RACHEL. Hey – we should celebrate!

NICK. Okay!

RACHEL. With dildos!

I start a temp job for the NHS. Not doing anything useful, not saving lives, just taking paid taxpayer money to do admin

Fiona still texts me, harrasses me daily about doing this... so in my smoke breaks I send Nick dildo pics.

NICK. Oh my days, can you –

RACHEL. Barrage him with them – links to harnesses on Amazon

NICK. Studded one's quite [nice] – hey STOP IT

RACHEL. Still got that butt plug, haven't you?

NICK. It's in a drawer

RACHEL. But you didn't get rid of it, did you?

NICK. ...I... didn't want Eddie to find it in the recycling. Look – we have a really fun thing going here...

RACHEL. Yeah, I agree, I'm offering you MORE fun, fuck it, we could make a whole weekend away of it! Get a hotel, I can wine and dine you before gently smashing your prostate?

NICK. Hold on I'm gonna – oh God I'm gonna come

RACHEL. Knew it

NICK. NOT cos of the –

RACHEL. You know if we pegged it would be, like, a *super* orgasm – life-ending orgasm – raise your ancestors from the dead kind of orgasm.

NICK. Yeah but like... I can just –

He comes.

You didn't – did you come?

RACHEL. Nah

NICK. Do you want me to... help you?

RACHEL. If I'm honest... the only times I've come in the last while... are when... I masturbate and think about pegging.

NICK. This has wormed deep into your psyche, hasn't it? Why!? Why *pegging?* I thought we – *you* said you didn't wanna do that?

RACHEL. I said I didn't wanna do it cos you said you didn't wanna do it but while you were saying you didn't wanna do it repeatedly it became clear to me that you desperately wanna do it, and now it's all I can think about all the time and I feel like if I don't peg I might die...

Eddie knocks at the – THIS IS POOR TIMING EDDIE

NICK *plays Eddie (through the door).*

NICK. Just wondered if you guys fancied dim sum?

RACHEL. Dim sum?

NICK. We could go to Ping Pong?

RACHEL. WE'RE BUSY

NICK....Okay, TTYL

To NICK*:*

RACHEL. What is his deal!?

NICK. He's hungry! SORRY MATE, NEXT TIME!

Beat.

RACHEL. What does Eddie say? About the pegging?

NICK. I haven't exactly –

RACHEL. You should tell him

NICK. No! No, no way

RACHEL. What, will he run off and tell all your friends? Go ask him

NICK. No!

RACHEL. Go ask him and I'll let this drop

NICK. Oh come on

RACHEL. Okay, *I'll* ask him

NICK. NO – no STOP

RACHEL. If you won't peg, I'll tell Eddie we pegged

NICK. What?

RACHEL. If we peg, I won't tell Eddie we pegged

NICK. That makes no sense

RACHEL. Do you think Eddie wants to peg?

NICK. HEY –

RACHEL. I'm joking, I get the feeling he doesn't wash his arse in the shower. Is that what this is? You're afraid what your friends will think

NICK. No – I mean, yeah I'd prefer we kept this between us but

RACHEL. What is it then? Really?

You know what, I promise I will stop bringing this up if you can actually tell me why, why you won't even entertain it

NICK. Look I'm... I'm... scared, okay? I'm scared

RACHEL. Of... me?

NICK. No, no of

RACHEL. Your mates – fuck 'em, who gives a shit what they think?

NICK. I do! I do, I... It's not that anyway it's not that. Like... what if it hurts or... I don't like it or

RACHEL. Okay. If it hurts, or you don't like it... then we stop. And I'll take care of you. And if you *do* like it...

And either way, I won't think of you any differently. I won't make fun of you or... does that help?

NICK. Yeah... yeah

RACHEL. One try, let's give it one little try

NICK. ...*Little* try?

Get It Done

RACHEL *and* NICK *unpack a weekend bag, packed to the brim with pegging equipment. They line up buttplugs, dildos, and a harness. A vat of gin. A vat of lube. They're being silly together, having a laugh.*

Maybe there's some kind of dalliance of them picking out equipment, NICK *being game, then freaking out as it gets to real, and backing off.* RACHEL *is patient throughout, reassuring him, but eventually we get the slightest hint she's getting impatient.*

Eventually, he can't go through with it. He collapses on the bed.

RACHEL. Always said we'd only do it if you wanted to do it

NICK. Yeah. I am... Really sorry, though

RACHEL. Listen, I'm over the moon with how this weekend's gone, I had the best steak of my life last night.

NICK. Ha, yeah. Proper nice here

RACHEL. Last time I had a weekend away… Was naaaaaat like this

NICK. I'll give you some money, for this

RACHEL. Honestly, you're fine, you don't owe me anything

NICK. Sure?

RACHEL. Yeah, my treat

Silence.

NICK. What was the weekend away?

RACHEL. Hm?

NICK. You said – last time you

RACHEL. Oh… Few years ago… My ex… Total arsehole

NICK. Ah. I never got to the… going away stage

RACHEL. Better off, trust me

Silence. She packs.

NICK. I mean, we're still gonna… we can still… Hang out… Right? I just think we've found our… cap? What's that?

RACHEL. Oh – hah – it's called Spider Man lube, look – it's like super… sticky and tacky

NICK. Oh weird! WHAAAAA

They play with it, doing the Spider Man hand flick. She reads the ingredients label.

RACHEL. Ooh, vegan

NICK. Thank God, cruelty free lube

RACHEL. Okay. That's everything. I'm gonna get some sleep if it's okay, train's at seven-forty-five

NICK. Yeah sure, sorry. And like. Sorry again

RACHEL. Honestly please stop saying sorry, you're fine. I don't, like, think any less of you

NICK. Sure okay good.

RACHEL. Seriously, I think it's brave you were willing to try, and brave you were able to say 'not for me' this weekend, okay? Your butthole, your choice. You were clear, you were honest. Trust me, that's refreshing.

NICK. Was your ex not...

RACHEL. Ugh, wanker.

NICK. Sure, sorry, course. Thanks, for being so, kind. About this.

RACHEL. No worries. Night.

She's about to go to bed, but pauses.

He cheated on me. We were together for three years, I thought it was all... Fine. Not perfect, nothing's perfect, you know. And then he... fucked my best mate. On my birthday. Said it was my fault

NICK. Your fault?!

RACHEL. Yeah, I was like, 'I'm sorry, did I stick *your* dick in someone else?' But he just went on about how he was bored, the spark was gone, he couldn't help it - –

NICK. Couldn't help it?

RACHEL. I'm a selfish, unloveable, stone cold bitch, apparently

NICK. Jesus...

RACHEL. Anyway, it all came out on this weekend away – he was trawling the apps as well, I found out... So it's been nice to actually have a good experience, replace the bad one. So thanks for that

NICK. Yeah. I'm so sorry

RACHEL. I mean, *you* didn't do it

NICK. Yeah, no, I mean... I guess... On behalf of mankind?

RACHEL. Ha, thanks. Okay. Sorry! Debbie Downer.

NICK. You're not… unloveable.

She kisses him on the top of the head.

RACHEL. Don't forget to set an alarm

NICK. Rach?

RACHEL. Yeah?

NICK. Quick before I change my mind

RACHEL. Quick what

NICK. QUICK PEG

RACHEL. What – really?

NICK. Yeah go on, fuck it, lube me up

RACHEL. Noooooo

NICK. Yeah, I'm serious, go go go

RACHEL. Okay – uh – towels

NICK. Towels?

RACHEL. Yeah, think its better if we… don't get shit on the bed

NICK. Sure, yes

RACHEL. I did actually take a pamphlet, hold on

NICK. You didn't

RACHEL. Yeah! Yeah – towels, lube, your butt should hopefully still be a bit… dilated from earlier

NICK. Great, great, definitely is, worryingly so

RACHEL. Do you wanna put some music on?

NICK. Okay –

RACHEL. I'll be right back

While she changes he reads the pamphlet. She reappears in lingerie.

NICK. Fuck, woah, you look AMAZING

RACHEL. Right! Thank you!

Okay.

NICK. Okay.

RACHEL. Okay, can you help me –

They struggle with the harness.

Hold on does it –

NICK. Which way does this –

RACHEL. Okay I've got instructions for this as well

NICK. Okay

They spend some time with the instructions.

Says the front is –

RACHEL. Ah yeah – here – got it. And then the –

They attach the dildo.

Oh – this is for me

She affixes a grinder to the harness. Another moment as they both take her in.

Ready?

NICK. Yeah. Wow it's real, it's happening

RACHEL. It's happening. You okay?

NICK. Yeah, yeah yeah, all good, terrified, all good

RACHEL. You can change your mind at any point, okay? Any point

NICK. Yeah, thanks, yeah

RACHEL. Is it just me or do I look unbelievably sexy in this?

NICK. You do and it really bothers me

RACHEL. Okay, lie down, breathe

Present yourself to me

NICK. Ahahahaha shiiiit, like this?

RACHEL. I'm joking, pamphlet says we actually want you on
your back for this. Firstly, so I can see the look on your face,
but secondly – probably more importantly – so you get to
control the angle and speed of entry, alright?

NICK. Does the pamphlet say anything about existential horror?

RACHEL. In the small print – also, importantly, as this is not
my dick, I can't, like, necessarily feel stuff, so you do need to
really steer me on what feels okay and what doesn't

NICK. Okay.

Right, like this?

RACHEL. Yep

NICK. You'll stop if I ask you to right?

RACHEL. Course – we're gonna go slow okay?

NICK. Okay

RACHEL. The second you don't like something you tell me,
okay?

NICK. Okay

RACHEL. Honestly anal kind of just feels like you're taking a
big satisfying shit again and again, like it's nice I promise

NICK. Ha, okay

RACHEL. We can stop anytime

NICK. Okay

RACHEL. Are you hyperventilating?

NICK. A bit

RACHEL. Okay, pause, pause pause pause

RACHEL *folds* NICK *into a hug and rocks him until his
breathing calms.*

We're doing this cos it's gonna be fun and feel nice and…
cos we trust each other. If it's not those things, we don't do it.

NICK. I'm just

I'm just getting in my head, you know? Like, suddenly, like, 'Oh my God what am I doing? Who am I? What if my mates find out and laugh at me? What if, I dunno, I shit myself? What if?'

RACHEL. Okay

They never need to know. And if they laugh at you it means they're pricks

And you might shit yourself, but you did douche earlier so we're *probably* okay, but if you do shit yourself, I won't judge you. Cos everybody shits.

NICK. Everybody shits

RACHEL. Everybody shits.

NICK. Okay. Thank you.

Okay. Let's do this

Pause.

RACHEL. Gonna just, get a bit of lube / on you

NICK. Ooooh cold, COLD

RACHEL. Okay? Ready? In three… two…

NICK. Let's not – let's not do a countdown

RACHEL. Sure. Remember I've got you so just… let go.

They peg, whatever that looks like on stage. The sillier the better. At first it's careful, worried.

All good?

NICK. Yeah, yep, yep, no going back now

Oh, okay, okay that feels – yeah okay – oooh, yeah

Then it's alright. Better than that, it's fun. Surprisingly fun.

She takes his hand.

Oh my God oh my God

RACHEL. Good, oh my God?

NICK. Good, oh my God Jesus

RACHEL. Oh my God

NICK. Fuck

RACHEL. Oh FUCK

NICK. Fuck

RACHEL. Fuck!

BOTH. FUUUUUUUUUUUUUUUUUUUUUUCK

*They both come extremely hard. They stare at each other,
eyes locked, both in a new kind of ecstasy.*

NICK. You look so –

RACHEL. I never noticed you had green eyes before

NICK. I saw my ancestors, you were right, I saw my ancestors,
right back to the dawn of time... and they were *really* proud
of me

They collapse back on the bed together.

PART TWO

Go Pikachu

Later that night. Darkness.

NICK. Rach? Rach, you asleep?

RACHEL. No. You?

NICK. No… I'm still buzzing

Can't believe we actually did it. Peg. And, like, I didn't disintegrate. After all that. If anything I've evolved – like a Pokemon

RACHEL. So… if Pikachu gets bummed it becomes like? –

NICK. Raichu

RACHEL. Upsettingly quick to answer that

NICK. I'm actually a massive nerd. Massive.

RACHEL. Oh God, I've really opened Pandora's box

NICK. Wait til I tell you about my Warhammer collection

RACHEL. Ahhhhhhhhhhahahaa that's *so lame*

NICK. Um, this coming from the woman *obsessed* with plastic food containers –

RACHEL. No, too far.

NICK. Sorry.

You were… *proper* sexy, you know. Looming over me

RACHEL. *Looming*?

NICK. No – I mean like, sexy looming, towering

RACHEL. Looming

NICK. Ignore that, I never said that. You enjoyed it though. Didn't you?

RACHEL. Yeah, yeah. It was great

Beat.

NICK. Can we do more of this?

RACHEL. Spooning? You know, this is the first time we've stayed the night since the first time

NICK. Oh yeah… We are doing it again, right?

RACHEL. Now?

NICK. No, no – when we get back. Like, generally. In the future

RACHEL. Oh, uh. Yeah, why not, yeah. Hadn't really thought about it

NICK. It's all I can think about, literally trying to sleep and my head's just like 'peg peg peg peg peg / peg peg'

RACHEL. Fuuuuck!

NICK. Peg peg peg peg / peg peg PEG PEG PEG PEG

RACHEL. Peg peg peg PEG PEG PEG PEG, loooooooool

NICK. So silly

RACHEL. *So* silly

Pegathon

Spring.

To us:

RACHEL. We skip work to peg

NICK. We don't really peg in public, too many logistical challenges

RACHEL. But we peg at my house. We peg at your house. And of course, we peg on my housemate's bed.

NICK. We peg morning, noon and night

RACHEL. We paint the town peg

NICK. We peg the house down

RACHEL. We go peg-wild

NICK. In for a penny, in for a peg

RACHEL. I'm a pegging machine

NICK. You can call me Peggy Sue

RACHEL. You want more?

NICK. Yeah

RACHEL. You want more?

NICK. Yeah!

RACHEL. Get on your knees

Next Level Peg

RACHEL*'s bedroom.*

RACHEL. Close your eyes!

NICK. Okay!

RACHEL. Eyes closed?

NICK. Yep! Hurry up!

　　RACHEL *is wearing insane thigh-high platform heels.*

RACHEL. Okay. Open.

NICK. Ho-ly. Shit.

RACHEL. You like it?

NICK. YES. Those. Are…

RACHEL. Not work appropriate

NICK. Ha! No

RACHEL. Imagine. Turn up to my temp job at Southwark Council like, 'THANKS FOR CALLING THE COUNCIL, YOU WORM, how can I help you today?'

NICK. Lol, like a weird sex line

RACHEL. 'Oh, your bins didn't get collected yesterday? Sorry to hear that – I WANNA SEE YOU LICK THEM CLEAN'

NICK. Fuuuuuck

Still kinda hot tho?

RACHEL. Yeah?

NICK. Yeah. Honestly you look amazing, let me look at you

RACHEL. On your knees

They peg, and both have a lovely time.

The next time:

Eyes closed!

NICK. They're closed they're closed! Come on!

RACHEL *is wearing a brand new, improved harness, and in her hands brandishes a couple of new, rather large, dildos.*

RACHEL. Okay. Open.

NICK. Oh!

RACHEL. You like them? Orange or pink?

NICK. Um… they look pretty uh… I don't know if I can take those yet

RACHEL. I reckon you can – I've got, like, an objective POV

NICK. What, on my arsehole?

RACHEL. Well yeah, I think she can take it

NICK. It's a she?

RACHEL. That just came out

NICK. I don't think she's a she

RACHEL. YOU just called her a she

NICK. HE isn't sure –

RACHEL. SHE needs to trust me

So!? Which one!

NICK. Um…. Er, orange, more manly

RACHEL. ON. YOUR. KNEES

They peg, and both have a lovely time.

NICK. OHmyGod

RACHEL. That okay?

NICK. More than okay, keep going

RACHEL. I. Am. Gonna. Destroy you.

NICK. OhmyGod you are *so* good at that

RACHEL. Yeah?

NICK. So terrifying

RACHEL. You are gonna RUE the day

NICK. Honestly ten out of ten, no notes

The next time:

RACHEL. Eyes closed?

NICK. Yes, Ma'am

RACHEL *struggles to pull on an insanely tight latex dress.*

RACHEL. Okay – I actually can't get this on…

NICK. What is it, what is it!?

RACHEL. Hold on, hold on…

RACHEL *Googles quickly.*

Be right back

Re-emerges with talcum powder, covers herself in it.

NICK. Rach?

RACHEL. Yeah, okay open, open, open, I can't get this – can you give me a hand?

RACHEL *struggles to heave the dress on.* NICK *opens his eyes.*

I can't –

NICK. Hold on, is this latex?

RACHEL. Yeah

NICK. Shit – I can't – I can't be near this

RACHEL. Shit? Really? I thought it was just – I didn't think you could be allergic to a whole dress -

NICK. Get it off get it off!

RACHEL. Shit! Oh my God!

She manages to pull it off, puts it outside.

Okay, it's gone, it's gone. I should shower, right? I'm so sorry, I wanted to be... extremely sexy and terrifying for you

NICK. I mean... in a way, you were. You could've, quite literally, destroyed me

Crushing Fantasy, But Make it Wholesome

Spooning:

NICK. I like this bit

RACHEL. Never saw myself being a big spoon

NICK. Never really did... hugs in my house. Just my dad, my brother and me.

RACHEL. Handshakes and fistbumps

NICK. Yeah. Don't get me wrong, we get on great. Three Musketeers. My brother's like, frustratingly successful. Nice cars and all that...

RACHEL. What about your mum?

NICK. She left. When I was ten

RACHEL. Oh

NICK. Yeah, we don't see her. Yeah it was... A rough few years.
Specially for my dad

RACHEL. That's shitty

NICK. Yeah

Silence.

I actually think this is my favourite bit. 'Aftercare'

RACHEL....Really?

NICK. Yeah. I mean, it's *all* great, don't get me wrong, but this
is... peak

Silence.

Do you think you could... Like, put a bit more welly into the
spooning?

RACHEL. Welly?

NICK. Yeah, so like at the moment it's giving... Holding
a newborn kitten... But I would love to feel... Like I'm
trapped inside an industrial car crushing machine, being
condensed into a tiny cube

Crushing fantasy, but make it wholesome

She spoons him, tight.

Yeah that's nice

Tighter.

Mmmm perfect

Tighter.

Oooh, ow! Hah! Rachel ow

Cut'n'run

Fiona and RACHEL *smoke outside a pub.*

NICK. Dump him

RACHEL. I can't just –

NICK. Dump him

RACHEL. I can't just… peg and dump!

NICK. Did he hate it?

RACHEL. *No* he fucking *loved* it

NICK. Really? Kind of thought it'd be more fun if he hated it a bit

RACHEL. Fiona you really need help –

NICK. Look he's catching feelings babe – he's imprinted on you

RACHEL. Like a duckling

NICK. Like a duckling. This isn't what you signed up for.

'Need help' – I'll have you know, we're in couples therapy

RACHEL. Oh!? Alright … How's that going?

NICK. I'm divorcing him

RACHEL. What???

NICK. I was going through his phone while he was in the shower – bastard had downloaded Tinder, so that was it for me. Threw a bowl of cereal at his head and told him we were finished.

RACHEL. I'm sorry?

NICK. Oh it's fine – I'm smashing it at work. Here – you dump that man and we can go absolutely rasher.

Two Hoots

A Pret A Manger.

NICK. Nice to be… out and about! For once. Isn't it? Nearly summer

RACHEL. Yeah! Yeah. So um, I wanted to –

NICK. I was gonna ask you something, actually

RACHEL. Oh! Okay

NICK. You go first

RACHEL. Oh um… No no. What were you? –

NICK. Yeah. Well. It's basically that I uh… I think we have loads of fun together –

RACHEL. Yeah, right

NICK. And the – the pegging has been… I mean, an unexpected… delight –

RACHEL. Yep yep yep

NICK. Yeah, great, so I was, I was actually talking to Eddie about you, not, like, details or anything, don't worry, but like, just what a good time we have…

And I was just telling him how I always sleep really well when we stay over, and he said he saw a TikTok, from, like, a therapist or something, saying that that means you actually feel really safe with the person, and…

And well, it's taken me a while to realise this, but what I wanted to bring up with you is that I think… I want more

RACHEL.…Honestly, short of taking a shit on your chest, I'm running flat out of ideas / at this point

NICK. Ha! No no no, sorry, of us, I mean. More of us.

RACHEL. Like a… boyfriend and girlfriend… heterosexual relationship?

NICK. Don't freak out –

RACHEL. I'm not freaking out, I'm not freaking out…

NICK. What did you wanna ask me, by the way?

RACHEL. Um… Let's circle back to that, sorry – Nick, we've never even… gone on a date?

NICK. I know, *exactly*, it's all been… a bit backwards, but I –

RACHEL. This was just sex, this was always just sex, *you* said that

NICK. I know, I know. But now I… Well, I guess you've found the way to my heart, and… turns out, it's through my butthole?

Okay in all seriousness, I mean, we've done… A lot… Together. And I… I wanna get to know *you*.

RACHEL. We do know each other?

NICK. Yeah, course, course, but not like… I don't even know your, like, favourite colour

RACHEL. Red – do you feel like you know me now?

NICK. That's not the – you know that's not the point. I mean, what kind of stuff do you… like?

RACHEL. Um – I dunno Netflix? Naps?

NICK. No… sport? Museums? Galleries? Anything like that?

RACHEL. Is that what you're into?

NICK. Yeah, I mean, yeah, I like being out and about

RACHEL. Beyoncé. I'm passionate about Beyoncé.

NICK. Really!?

RACHEL. What do you mean, 'really'? She's *Be-yon-cé*

NICK. She's overrated

RACHEL. EXCUSE ME?

NICK. Sorry, sorry… But she is, right?

RACHEL. See!? We could never –

NICK. Okay ignore that, ignore that! I'm messing we've got loads in common, we get on like a house on fire… I mean… I care about you…

Is that… A 'no' then?

RACHEL. I just… I really wasn't expecting

NICK.…Why… did you want to meet up with me?

RACHEL. Um… Hah… Not sure how to say this now, but…

NICK. Hold on, hold on, hold on… No. No??? No way… Were you gonna break up with me… in a Pret?

RACHEL. No, I was gonna do it on the street but you wanted a hoisin duck wrap, so…

NICK. Oh, fuck

RACHEL. I'm sorry! I just felt like… We'd reached the end of the road… A *great* road

NICK. Oh fuck, *idiot*

RACHEL. And we could amicably be like… thank you for some lovely orgasms… goodbye?

Are you…

NICK. Not crying, *not* crying – I actually can't properly cry, my tearducts don't really produce… I trained them out of it, years of repression, so I, I just make… crying faces

RACHEL. Oh my God, I'm sorry, I'm really sorry. You look hilarious, I'm sorry

NICK. Stoooooop

RACHEL. I think you're great too, I really do. You're a hoot!

NICK. We have such a hoot together

RACHEL. I know, *such* a hoot

NICK. We could have more hoots though! I want *more*

RACHEL. I don't know how much hoot I have left in me

NICK. Rachel *this* is why I'm so into you

RACHEL. I'm hilarious, I'm a catch, I know, it's okay, it's okay

NICK. You are though, you really are

He gathers himself.

Can I say one thing?

RACHEL. Yeah

NICK. Look at me. I am not your ex.

RACHEL....

NICK. I would *never, ever* do that to you. I would *never* cheat on you. I would never intentionally hurt you.

I swear to you, I am a good egg. Let me prove that to you.

...Are *you* crying?

RACHEL. Nope, no, I look like Kim Kardashian when I cry, I can't do that here –

NICK. Force it down, force it down

Together, they clench their fists and RACHEL *forces her emotions back down.*

RACHEL. Okay

NICK. Okay?

RACHEL. Okay. Are you gonna finish that wrap?

NICK. It's yours.

So, can I... take you on a date?

No strap-ons, no costume, just...

RACHEL. Us... staring at each other

NICK. Maybe with pizza?

RACHEL. Fuck it, I'm in.

Whips and Chains

Summer.

To us:

RACHEL. We go to M&Ms world

NICK. To admire the wall of M&Ms this time

RACHEL. We do a pottery class in Clapham

NICK. We play crazy golf in Shoreditch

RACHEL. We do axe-throwing in Hammersmith

NICK. We do an Alcatraz escape room in Vauxhall

RACHEL. We do a Harry Potter immersive experience in Hackney

NICK. We go for dinner at Nandos

RACHEL. Wagamama

NICK. Wahaca

RACHEL. Giggling Squid

NICK. KFC

RACHEL. Five Guys

NICK. Giraffe

RACHEL. Pizza Express

NICK. YO! Sushi

RACHEL. Slug and Lettuce

NICK. Las Iguanas

RACHEL. Gourmet Burger Kitchen

NICK. Turtle Bay

RACHEL. Bella Italia

NICK. Zizzi

RACHEL. ASK Italian

NICK. Prezzo

RACHEL. McDonald's

NICK. Wetherspoons

RACHEL. Chicken Cottage

NICK. And… Spudulike

RACHEL. We do grocery shops at Tesco

NICK. We do the dishes

RACHEL. We text each other 'morning, beautiful'

NICK. That's my favourite bit, cos I feel beautiful for the whole day

RACHEL. We binge Netflix

NICK. With Eddie!

RACHEL. He commentates throughout

NICK. His favourite show is *Too Hot to Handle*

RACHEL. You need to tell Eddie to stay in his room or…I will bang you with the Mistress Twister

NICK. Not sure that's a fair punishment. Can the Mistress Twister *not* be a part of this relationship?

RACHEL. She'll always be part of this relationship, she hangs over us like a shadow.

NICK. We're in a thruple with the Mistress Twister

RACHEL. If anything, I'm in a relationship with with the Mistress Twister, and you're just… here

NICK. We're in a thruple with Eddie

RACHEL. NO, no we are not in a thruple with Eddie

NICK. We reach the point where we openly wear our retainers in front of each other

RACHEL. I get period stains on his sheets

NICK. She holds my hair back while I vomit after too many beers

RACHEL. He helps me send out CVs to get a proper fucking job with a salary and sick pay

NICK. She helps me prep for my interview for this permanent job I've been tapped on the shoulder for

RACHEL. We go to galleries and I have mixed feelings about it

NICK. She points at all the paintings and goes, 'I could do that'

RACHEL. I reckon I could, and if I could do it, it's not art.

NICK. She pops pimples on my back

RACHEL. I've never felt more satisfied or fulfilled than when I pop his pimples, it's better than sex

NICK. We hold hands

RACHEL. We hold hands

NICK. I tell you all about my family, my brother, my dad, my mum leaving, my first teenage girlfriend, the lads' holidays I've gone on, the best meals I've ever eaten, the way that for some reason, and I know it's weird, but my favourite dessert is bread and butter pudding

RACHEL. Soggy things, you seem to like soggy textured things?

And don't get me wrong. We're still pegging like the clappers.

How do you feel about names?

NICK. Like pet names?

RACHEL. No, like, in a session, like, if I called you 'Lil' Bitch'

NICK. Lil' Bitch?

RACHEL. Sounds like a shit rapper doesn't it, Lil' Kim, Lil' Bitch

NICK. Yeah, it doesn't... doesn't do it for me

Do I look like a Lil' Bitch? When we're doing it?

RACHEL. No! No. No. Course not, no. No. Kind of.

   I buy the Mistress Twister.

   RACHEL*'s flat*.

NICK. You bought the Mistress Twister

RACHEL. Yeah!

NICK. You *bought* the Mistress Twister

RACHEL.… Yeah… Just for fun! Bit of craic. Just for the display cabinet

   Okay will we, uh – don't worry I've got a reasonably sized one –

NICK. I actually – I got us tickets to this uh… comedy thing

RACHEL. Oh, uh, I thought – really?

NICK. Yeah it's like a gong show thing – bunch of comedians have to make it to five minutes without getting booed off

   Should be fun!

RACHEL. It's just we… Haven't done it in a while

NICK. Haven't we?

RACHEL. You're still enjoying it, right?

NICK. Oh yeah, hundred per cent

RACHEL. You're not bored, are you?

NICK. NO – God no. Just enjoying… Getting to know you

LOL

The Comedy Store, off Leicester Square.

RACHEL. What?

NICK. What?

RACHEL. Why do you keep looking at me – watch the stage

NICK. Shhh, they'll pick on us if they see us talking

RACHEL. Then stop looking at me, you little creeper

NICK. How do you know I'm looking if you're so focused on the stage?

RACHEL. I have peripheral vision, babe.

NICK. This is fun, isn't it?

RACHEL. Shhhhh

NICK. You'd be great up there, you know

RACHEL. Room full of people staring at me, no thanks

Plus, this is literally a parade of white guys making jokes about incest and paedophilia. Wouldn't fit in.

NICK. Some of them were funny

RACHEL. Seriously?

NICK. They're being ironic

RACHEL. Did you not notice that every woman that gets up there doesn't make it a minute before the red cards go up?

NICK. Not all of them!

RACHEL. Yeah, the old lady made it because she's basically completely unthreatening and no one expected her to be any good

NICK. But she *was* good

RACHEL. They've all been good, they just wouldn't give them a chance. It's like a braying mob in here, like a medieval town square

NICK. It's meant to be a bit... mercenary

RACHEL. It's like we're in The Upside Down

NICK. Well yeah, exactly, we get to come out, sink a few beers, be a bit mean or shouty or whatever, then go home and forget about it

Will we go? There's a Shake Shack near the –

RACHEL. No, no… I am actually quite enjoying it, annoyingly. Just – eyes forward

Do you really think… I'd be good at it?

NICK. God yeah, you'd be brilliant

RACHEL. Ha, completely dominate the crowd

NICK. No, like, as you. Just you.

LOL JK

Shake Shack, later that night.

NICK. I'll get this, by the way. My treat

RACHEL. I don't mind we can split / it if you –

NICK. No no no no honestly, I'd really like to

RACHEL. Thanks

NICK. So… I was thinking –

RACHEL. Sketch group!

NICK. Ha, no – I was actually thinking about what I'd say, like, if I did comedy

RACHEL. The world *really* needs another white, male comedian

NICK. Ha, true true. I'm not gonna do it, I was just thinking about it, like, what would I say… Sorry, stupid

RACHEL. No no

NICK. I've always thought it was really weird the way self-checkouts at supermarkets, when you're done, they like scream at you 'PLEASE TAKE YOUR ITEMS'

RACHEL.…

NICK. It's like, yeah, obviously! I'm not gonna buy them, you know pay for them and then just like, leave them there

RACHEL....

NICK. Just seems really dumb. Like I wanna scream at them 'NO I... WANNA LEAVE MY ITEMS'

Hah – '*YOU* TAKE YOUR ITEMS' Need to work on a punchline

RACHEL. Yeah, yeah... there's something there

NICK. Or I was thinking I could like, if I was gonna talk about myself I'd like... do some Mum-abandoned-me jokes

RACHEL. Damnnnn. Don't most people do... usually dating stories isn't it?

NICK. Hah, yeah. This one girl I met up with, honestly her pictures were like, it turned out they were of her friend, not her

RACHEL. Oh shiiit

NICK. Yeah, and she was... [larger]

RACHEL. I went on this date, years ago, before my ex, and this guy's pictures were kind of cute, and he seemed funny – he was a comedy writer. And I'm waiting for him outside the bar, and the second he turned up I was like *oh damn,* I could *never* bang you. And then, we were literally *one drink in,* when he goes like 'Oh, I think parents who don't send their kids to private school obviously don't love their kids enough'

NICK. *What?*

RACHEL. Yeah, cos he was like 'If they loved them, they'd just work harder, wouldn't they? So they have the money to send them to private school.'

NICK. Woooooooow

RACHEL. Then we went to this other bar –

NICK. Hold on – you *stayed!?*

RACHEL. Yeah

NICK. Why?

RACHEL.…Cos… I didn't wanna be rude?

> We're walking past this Indian restaurant, and he starts
> telling me he went there once, years ago, and the food wasn't
> very good, but he got so drunk that night he got sick, and it
> actually tasted way better on the way out –

NICK. That's so bleak

RACHEL. Literally told me he enjoyed the taste of his own
vomit

NICK.…You left at this point, right?

RACHEL. No

NICK. *NO*?

RACHEL. Cos I'm *nice*! And *then* at the end of the date, I need
to get the train home cos I've got work in the morning, and
he keeps being like: 'Come on, stay out, let's go clubbing' –
it's a Tuesday – 'You can stay at mine – stay on my couch'
– I'm like *mate,* I wasn't born *yesterday*

> So finally I'm like, okay fuck being nice, I've said three
> times I'm not going clubbing, so I say, 'Listen, seriously, I'm
> going home.'

> And then he turns to me, dead serious, and he's like: 'I just
> spent fifty quid on you.'

> That's the… that was meant to be the punchline. Ha, needs
> punching up, obviously. I've got a *lot* of dating stories

> You okay?

NICK. Sorry, no I… just feel bad. That's really shitty

RACHEL. No honestly, it's fine, it was funny, it's funny, it's just
a shit date, I mean, there's *way* worse

> This one guy shows up, he's so small I could roll him in a
> cigarette, which he had *not* disclosed. But again, I stay, to
> be nice. And afterwards, we're both about to go through the
> barriers at Liverpool Street and he's like, 'Text me when you

get home safe! Or, I dunno, text your friends or something.'
Sure. Then he goes, 'Cool, cool, yeah I'll text my friends to
let them know I didn't like rape you or whatever.'

NICK. *What?!*

RACHEL. Yeah. And like, later he text me and I had to be like:
'Yeah, by the way, best not to make jokes about raping a
woman you've just met?' And he's like, 'Yeah, sorry, when
I'm nervous, stuff just comes out.'

And part of me's like, okay, fair enough, nerves, whatever.
But then part of me's like, well, the scary thing is that it's *in
there*. Like, it slipped out cos *it's in your head.*

Again, usually gets a bigger laugh when I tell it, but

Sorry, really didn't mean to… put a massive downer on this

NICK. No, no it's fine

RACHEL. Start to wonder sometimes, like, is it me? Do I have
this… vibe… that just attracts, like, awful people? Not you –
I don't mean you – I know you're not like that.

You Stole My Heart

Middle of the night, whispered.

RACHEL. Nick?

Nick, you asleep?

NICK. No. You?

RACHEL. No

NICK. You okay?

RACHEL. Yeah

Yeah

I need to tell you something

NICK. Okay

    You can tell me anything

RACHEL. Yeah?

    Promise?

NICK. Yeah

RACHEL. Okay.

    All I can think about is shoplifting

NICK. WHAT?

RACHEL. Yeah, I tried it for the first time a few weeks ago, now I'm hooked

NICK. Seriously?

RACHEL. Yeah, can't get enough

    Am I a bad person?

NICK. No! Kind of

RACHEL. Yeah

NICK. Why?

RACHEL. Skincare's really expensive

NICK. You're stealing skincare?

RACHEL. Yeah, there's no other way I can stay looking youthful

NICK. There literally is

RACHEL. I just feel like, if I can just use *enough* of her products, I too can look like Rihanna. To be clear, I would *never* steal from an independent or a small business

NICK. Oh, okay

RACHEL. Only huge corporations

NICK. Ethical theft

RACHEL. That's less bad, right?

NICK. ...Are you short on money?

RACHEL. No, no

 I mean like... the job search is killing my soul, but

 It's more that like, I actually saw someone else doing it – it got me irrationally angry, cos this woman was like, really obvious about it, just like, looked around and put a handful of nail polishes in her bag and I was like – are you for real? You're just gonna... take those?

NICK. So... you concluded that... *you* should do it

RACHEL. Yeah... I just wanted to try it, see if it was actually that easy

 And it is, I mean, for me

 I mean, I feel like I can't go into Boots ever again cos they probably have reams of footage of me stealing moisturisers. But... so far... scot-free.

 I told you, bad person

NICK. ...Maybe I should try it

RACHEL. You should, you're looking a little crusty

NICK. Hey!

 You know there's this thing with putting cameras over self-checkouts, so you can see yourself – if you feel watched you're less likely to do bad stuff

RACHEL. Not me

NICK. ...That's what you wanted to tell me?

RACHEL. Yeah

NICK. Did you think I was gonna, like, condemn you?

RACHEL. No. Yeah. Maybe. You should. I'm a criminal now

NICK. Yeah, a criminal with *amazing* skin

RACHEL. Rotten on the inside but absolutely glowing on the outside

NICK. What happened to Tupperware?

RACHEL. I know. Just wasn't scratching the itch any more

NICK. Are you gonna stop?

RACHEL. I want to but... I don't know if I can even control myself around cosmetics any more

NICK. I fucking love you, you know that?

RACHEL....

NICK....

RACHEL....

NICK. You could almost say –

RACHEL. Don't say it –

NICK. You *could* say –

RACHEL. Don't you fucking dare say it –

NICK. You stole my heart.

RACHEL. Fuck. Ruined it.

I could never love you

NICK. I'd actually understand

Sorry though, that was... not planned. But... I think I do, actually?

RACHEL. You're in love with a very immoral person

NICK. I think that's the bit I'm most into?

RACHEL. I did not see this conversation going this way. I'm gonna have to steal a gift for you now

NICK. Can it be an Xbox?

RACHEL. Yeah. You're the only person I'd thieve for

NICK. So silly

RACHEL. *So* silly

NICK. Come here. You're gonna have to work very hard to make me hate you, you know that, right?

> RACHEL *tries to look away but* NICK *takes her face, and looks into her eyes.*

> *Interval.*

Daddy Issues

Autumn.

Some kind of post-interval number to get us back in. The following montage as a ditty.

To us:

RACHEL. We go to barbeques

NICK. Brunches

RACHEL. I tell so many people their ugly babies are adorable, yes *definitely* gorgeous, I know, everyone says that about their kids but yours *definitely* are, definitely are

NICK. A kink event in Kings Cross

RACHEL. It gets too much, we leave

NICK. Latex everywhere

RACHEL. A food festival at Hampton Court

NICK. I ask Eddie if he wants to come but –

RACHEL. *Thankfully* he's keeping to himself these days

NICK. A music festival in Victoria Park

RACHEL. We do a shedload of mandy

NICK. Scream and cry at each other about how in love we are

RACHEL. We're having a hoot

NICK. Never were more hoots had

RACHEL. Then, September, it's my birthday and Nick goes all
out. We get the ferry over to Greenwich and look at Cutty
Sark. Go round the markets, pub lunch. Get back to mine and
he's got me presents: a pair of earrings in the shape of squids,
and a… Swan lilo?

Rachel's flat:

NICK.…For our holiday

RACHEL. Fuck *oooooff* nooooooo

NICK. Yes! I booked us a holiday to…

RACHEL. The / Maldives

NICK. Belfast

RACHEL. Belfast?

NICK. Yeah! …*Game of Thrones*!!!!

RACHEL. Ohhhh

NICK. We can sit on the Iron Throne! And, I thought, we could
get the bus down and see some of your family in Dublin???

RACHEL. Yeah… Yeah! Amazing! Iron Throne, you absolute
nerd, amazing, thank you!

To us:

My phone goes off –

NICK. Do you wanna get that?

RACHEL. No no no it's fine it's no one

NICK. Not some… mysterious man you're seeing

RACHEL. NO, no, God no – here, will we get Deliveroo?

To us:

Bit later, I leave the room to wee and… phone goes off again.
Nick answers it

NICK. Sorry – it was your dad… Wanted to know if we wanted
to come for a drink? I can get us an Uber there, if you –

RACHEL. Um… No. No. I'd… really rather not

NICK. Oh okay. Are you sure? I'd love to meet him –

RACHEL. I *really* would rather not

NICK. Do you wanna talk about it?

RACHEL. No

NICK. Okay

To us:

RACHEL. We watch *Married at First Sight*. I love trash TV cos
it's a safe forum to ruthlessly judge people.

To each other:

NICK. What does your dad do?

RACHEL. He's retired

NICK. What did he used to do?

RACHEL. He was a CEO. Some company in Canary Wharf.
Finance-type stuff

NICK. You two get on?

RACHEL. Spanish inquisition over here!

NICK. Sorry! Just… curious

RACHEL. Yeah, we do… Some of the time. Up and down.

And then he arrives. Turns up at the door. Tanked.

Which is not… A one-off occurrence. I mean, I have this
kind of, spidey-sense, that can tell the second he's even had
the whiff of a drink, but this is… he's off the deep end…

RACHEL *tries to work up to continue telling the story but
struggles.*

To RACHEL, *but 'outside' of the play –*

NICK. Will I… [tell it]?

RACHEL. Um… No, no, I can [do it]

She hesitates

NICK. I can do it? I'll do it… If you [want]

RACHEL. Um. Yeah, okay, okay

To us:

NICK. So Finbarr hammers on the door, yelling that if we won't go for a drink with him, he'll come to us, cos it's a Friday night, and we're no craic, and no daughter of his is going to be a dryshite

Rachel's up like a shot -

'In' the scene:

RACHEL. You can go, I'll deal with this, you can go –

NICK. No, it's fine, I'll stay, I'm staying

RACHEL. Please, *please* can you go?

NICK. It's fine, let me help!

To us:

And he's like, barrelling around, searching the cupboards for drink

To each other, 'in' the scene:

RACHEL. Get him a drink – get him a drink

NICK. Surely that's – make it worse?

RACHEL. Trust me, what's worse is if you tell him 'no'

To us:

NICK. She's calling her mum

To each other, 'in' the scene:

RACHEL. Fuck's sake, she's saying there's nothing she can do
– there's never *anything* she can do, just says wait for him to
pass out on the couch

NICK. Do you want me to kick him out?

RACHEL. NO, no, no please can you just fucking leave? Please
fuck off, please?

NICK. I can't leave you here with –

RACHEL. He'll run out of steam, he just wants to drink and list
his regrets and whine about how he 'used to be someone', it's
stupid, that's how this goes

NICK. ...Okay... will we let him run out of steam, together?

RACHEL. I *wish* you'd fucking leave

NICK. I'm *not* going.

To us:

So we sit. In the living room. With the Live Laugh Love
poster. And drink gin and tonics. She won't sit near me.

Finbarr rambles, demands we put music on. Briefly sings,
briefly gets up and dances...

I chat to him, try and make nice, ask him questions - he loves
that - goes all in giving me the 'dad' treatment: 'What are
your intentions with my daughter?'

He keeps trying to get her up dancing, to get her to talk, to
laugh. I've tried, I've really tried to keep him sweet, steer the
conversation... But the more she doesn't engage the angrier
he gets and eventually he just lets her have it –

'We should've stayed in Ireland but no, you, *you* had to go
to your special arts school, your mother *insisted* we bring
you here, ship you around to all your lessons, thousands and
thousands in fees, recitals – JAYSUS recitals til your eyes
would bleed, and then... What? You just... decide you don't
like it any more? And you just... quit?

'No wonder you're broke, living with some stranger, spending your nights with this thick. You're useless. You're tedious. You know, you could've actually been something, if you'd only worked for it. I'll tell you what, you're hard work Rachel you're hard work –

'I told the last one, hah, I told your man, she's *hard work* my Rachel, I don't know where we got her, and he knew it, oh he was out of there like a shot, lucky escape. You'd wanna take notes, fella –'

She doesn't move, but I'm up, and I've shoved him out of the living room, practically carry him out the door before he has time to process what I'm doing and fight back.

He's gone.

She's still sat in the exact same spot. I've never seen her like this. Small.

A beat as he takes her in. She is childlike. Numb.

To RACHEL, *'in' the scene:*

Rachel? Look at me?

Rachel? He didn't mean that

RACHEL. I know. He's always been a drunk.

NICK. Exactly, it's not your fault... Rachel?

RACHEL. No don't [touch me]

Doesn't even know it's my birthday. Just wanted a drinking buddy.

NICK. I'm so sorry...

RACHEL. I'm going to bed.

NICK. I'll come –

RACHEL. No, can you – can you sleep in my housemates room, I just need

NICK. Will she –

RACHEL. I don't care, I'm moving out anyway

NICK. What?

RACHEL. She got engaged so she's kicking me out.

I'm going to bed

I'll understand if you um, if you're not here in the morning.

NICK. Rachel –

She closes the bedroom door.

Deep breath. It's over.

To NICK, *but 'outside' of the scene,* RACHEL *mouths, 'Thank you.'*

Peg for Your Life

To us:

RACHEL. I start flat-hunting, interviewing to be a housemate, telling everyone I'm fun! But clean. Great craic! But also quiet. They turn me down, they all turn me down, cos for every decently priced room about eight million people apply and – *get on your knees –*

NICK. Are you okay? You seem / tense –

RACHEL. Get on your –

NICK. Do you wanna / talk about it?

RACHEL. I'm temping at Camden Council in Adult Social Care, where the head of department has me spend my days printing out his emails, so he can write – in pen – his response on them – and then hand them back to me to email the replies, which say – *on your knees – no, that way –*

NICK. Can we – I like looking at you, when we –

RACHEL. I *said...* on your knees

NICK. I like when we can see each other, make eye contact

RACHEL. ON YOUR FUCKING –

NICK. Where are you going?

RACHEL. I've got an interview tomorrow morning so I wanna be at home, you know, get ready and stuff

NICK. But... who'll hold me like a baby?

RACHEL. On your –

NICK. My knees actually hurt a bit lately... Might need knee pads or something

Lots of overlapping in the next:

RACHEL. ON YOUR –

NICK. Look, can we talk about – with your Dad / it must've been –

RACHEL. It has nothing to do with him, / I'm fine –

NICK. Really / upsetting –

RACHEL. This is nothing to do with that, / don't make it about that –

NICK. We haven't talked about it / at all –

RACHEL. It's not about that and I don't like you linking it / to that, I'm fine

NICK. And you've been / really – [unwell]... ever since

RACHEL. I told you I'm fine and you're trying to shame me –

NICK. No no no I'm not – I promise I'm not –

RACHEL. I've started running, taken up running, I've heard about 'runner's high', haven't experienced it yet, I'm sure I will, my joints ache, I'm a runner now – *you worthless, worthless piece of shit –*

NICK. Sorry – Rach? Rach, can you untie me?

RACHEL. Stop whining, you little *bitch*

NICK. No, sorry – it actually hurts –

RACHEL. It's meant to

NICK. No like, *bad* hurts

RACHEL....Fine

NICK. You can stay over? Why do you never wanna stay over anymore?

I Just Want Normal, Straightforward, Passionless, Expressionless, Perfunctory Sex

The bedroom.

RACHEL. Don't be afraid to come

Nick? Don't be afraid to let go

NICK. I'm... I'm... I'm not gonna come

I'm not really... Can we stop a sec?

RACHEL. What's going on?! There was a time when you were, literally pegging-*mad*.

NICK. Yeah. Yeah I know. I kind of wondered, like lately I've been thinking about

We don't really have... normal sex any more

RACHEL. Normal?

NICK. Yeah, no I mean... This is all we do. I miss – I'd like to, you know, have sex with you sometimes as well

RACHEL. Fuck me?

NICK. Sure, okay, fuck you, whatever you want to call it, penetrate you, make love to you, put / my dick in you, I dunno

RACHEL. Yeah I get it I get it

NICK. Just feels like… Bit one sided these days

RACHEL. I thought you loved it

NICK. I do, yeah I do

RACHEL. I'm embarrassed now

NICK. No – I wasn't trying to – that's not

RACHEL. I really thought you liked this and I thought you liked it cos I like it

NICK. I do, I do – hey – where / are you

RACHEL. It's fine I just need – I'm just gonna go for a smoke

NICK. Okay – I didn't mean to – I wasn't trying to upset you I just wanted to… talk about

I wondered if maybe we should even maybe… stop having sex. For a while, just for –

RACHEL. Why?

NICK. Just… Take a breather… Spend some time together… it was just a thought!

Rachel? Look at me? Look, things've been really off since / your dad –

RACHEL. I'm going for a smoke.

NICK.…I love you?

Till Death

NICK*'s brother's wedding day.*

To us:

RACHEL. I like weddings. In principle. I like love. It's nice to celebrate love. I like drinking. I like dressing up. I like a free meal. Not a fan of the institution of marriage. Not a fan of the church. Not a fan of kids at weddings. But what I *hate* is having to splash out on an Airbnb or hotel for the weekend, transport, a new outfit, new shoes, a wedding present and I HATE HATE HATE when, after all that, they don't have an open bar.

NICK. It's my brother Stephen's wedding. I'm best man. I'm so proud of him.

RACHEL. It's that bit, after the ceremony, where the couple's taking photos, so everyone's hanging around, cold, starving, and harrassing the wait staff to top up their prosecco. I'm drunk, but worse, I'm hangry.

NICK. Everyone says they're very impressed I've managed to bag a tall lady, by the way. They approve.

RACHEL. Oh they approve. Great.

Eddie's been hanging around Nick and I like a bad fucking smell. I have to say it: he's got incel vibes.

NICK. My dad, Len's a retired train driver, also nervously hanging around us cos there are a *lot* of fancy looking people here.

As Len:

Well, lovely to finally meet you Rachel! Sorry, I'm a bit maudlin today, days like this always remind you of your own wedding. Maybe it'll be you two next, eh?

RACHEL. Oh yeah, well this one certainly wants to be… tied down

NICK. Oh aye? On the cards then?

RACHEL. Oh yeah, *loves* getting on his knees – one knee

As NICK:

NICK. Rach!?

RACHEL. What?

As Len:

NICK. She's a firecracker this one – I like you

RACHEL. Len – you've got me pegged

As NICK:

NICK. Rach can we have a / word?

RACHEL. Babe! I'm chatting to your dad, don't be a lil bitch!

NICK. Stop it – Dad, give us a minute

RACHEL *lamps a drink back.*

You wanna slow down on those?

RACHEL. This is the only free drink we get today we gotta get our money's worth

NICK. You're really on one today, what's going on with you?

RACHEL. I'm just having a bit of fun!?

NICK. That's my *Dad*

RACHEL. Lighten up, he's got no idea! You're so sensitive

NICK. Can you just… Tone it down? Be nice, make friends?

RACHEL. I am making friends! Your dad's a bit of a Debbie Downer though eh? See why your mum chucked in the towel

NICK.…

RACHEL. That's a joke –

NICK. Not fucking funny

RACHEL. It was a – he storms off.

But guess who's still lurking? Eddie. FUCK OFF EDDIE! WHY WON'T YOU EVER JUST FUCK OFF? You're like a fucking *child*

Bit later, I'm hiding round the back of a flowery trellis thing, smoking, trying to call Fiona who's not picking up – when I realise there's people behind me chatting – on the other side. Eddie… and Nick.

RACHEL *plays Eddie*.

NICK. I don't know why she's being like this! Today!
Especially today!

RACHEL. Mate, she's *always* like this

NICK. I mean she – no she isn't – she is – / not always –

RACHEL. She is mate, trust me, I know a psycho when I see
one –

NICK. Okay, I have to tell someone this, I… you know the stag?

RACHEL. What happens on the stag, stays / on the

NICK. I kissed… this girl…

RACHEL. Maaaate

NICK. Yeah – it was the end of the night – it was just a kiss – I
was high, drunk and high – and she was … Fuck it she was
just… *nice to me?* So I kissed her… Rachel doesn't even
really… kiss me?

RACHEL. You've got to chuck her, mate

NICK. I just don't know if… You know her dad's like… a
horrendous alcoholic.

RACHEL. There you go

NICK. And she's got some ex who *she says* cheated on her –

RACHEL. I mean, basically a template feminazi with daddy
issues – bet she doesn't shave her armpits either, am I right?
Do you believe her?

NICK. I dunno, I mean, yeah, but then *now* I'm just. I'm starting
to wonder if… he saw something I haven't? And jumped ship
just in time. When someone has enough car crash stories, you
start to be like… Maybe *you're* the common denominator
here?

Whipping Boy

Later, the hotel room.

RACHEL*'s extremely drunk. She aggressively pins* NICK *to the wall and makes out with him. He gently pushes her away.*

RACHEL. What, don't you wanna fuck me any more?

NICK. No, no no course not, you're just a bit... Drunk, that's all

RACHEL. Oh, you're so good. So noble. Such a *nice guy*

NICK. Here, do you wanna lie down? You'll feel / better in the –

RACHEL. NO, I don't wanna lie down – I am gonna fuck you *senseless* – you little bitch –

She's managed to get his belt off, tries to playfully whack it on the edge of the bed.

NICK. Can we just –

RACHEL. Don't worry, they won't hear us – your secret's safe with me

She tries to playfully whip him on the bum with the belt, but it's clumsy, uncomfortable.

Oh your knees, sweetcheeks

NICK. No I really – honestly – Rach? I think I'm at my limit. With this

RACHEL. ...With me?

NICK. No – no – with... with... pegging – all *this* stuff

RACHEL. What? This is what you wanted, you *love* –

NICK. Any more. Any more. I'm not. I don't wanna do it any more. If that's okay. I want *you* – but I don't –

RACHEL. You've gotta be fucking kidding me – this is a play, it's got to be a play –

NICK. I'm not –

RACHEL. No, you don't get to – get on your knees

NICK. I'm not – no

She snaps the belt against the bed again.

RACHEL. I said ON YOUR FUCKING KNEES

She tries to get him on his knees, drunk, clumsy.

NICK. Come on, Rach

RACHEL. I know this is what you want

NICK. For fuck's sake, Rachel – stop it

RACHEL. NO – NOW BEND OVER YOU – YOU FUCKING
    MAGGOT, YOU FUCKING SIMP

NICK. Rachel –

RACHEL. *You* don't get to tell me 'No,' *you* don't get to take it
    for *weeks* – for months – like a little bitch – begging me for
    it, banging on about it the whole time, telling me how much
    you love it, how much you love me and then turn around tell
    me 'No.' There's something really fucking wrong with you,
    you know that?

NICK. No, I'm done, I'm not into this any more, no, done.

RACHEL. Done?

NICK. Done. With that. Not us. But that. No.

Silence.

Then RACHEL *whacks and whacks and whacks the bed post
with the belt, whacks and whacks and whacks, roaring.*

Rachel!? Rachel!!!!

She shoves him

RACHEL. NO – you don't get to –

NICK. Calm down – Jesus, you're hysterical

RACHEL. HYSTERICAL?

She shoves him again.

RACHEL. NO

NICK. Can't we just – look this isn't going to fix the –

RACHEL. You fucking prick

NICK. Let's just talk about it –

RACHEL. I don't want to fucking talk about it! I don't want to
– fuck you! FUCK YOU!

NICK. Rachel I'm not saying –

RACHEL. I know what you're saying! I know exactly what
you're saying! I did this for *you*, I did this cos *you* wanted to
do it –

NICK. That's not – you said you –

RACHEL. Bought all this stuff – acted like a – the amount of
stuff I did for you! That I didn't want to!

NICK. What? What stuff?

RACHEL. Cos you you push and push and push and push and
nag and whine and and I don't know who I fucking *am* any
more

Silence.

NICK. I know who you are – *you* know who you are –

RACHEL. Don't look at me – *stop looking at me*

NICK. Rachel this isn't – I'm not –

RACHEL. You know what my favourite part is? The bit that
really gets me going? It's not the pegging, it's not hearing
you fucking whimper as I slide into you, it's afterwards, it's
looking at you all curled up, covered in your own come,
shivering, looking doe-eyed at me – you look so so so – so
fucking *weak*

NICK. Rachel, that's not… That's not fair

RACHEL. You fucking piece of shit

She shoves him again. He catches her wrists this time.

You look… Like a little. Bitch.

Disgusting. And weak.

Beat.

Then… she starts to laugh.

Really cackle, right in his face.

Just like that, he's counteracted her force, overpowered her and she's on the floor.

To be clear, this shouldn't look like an act of violence in and of itself, neither of them are physically hurt, the goal is demonstrating that ultimately, he is stronger than her, he COULD overpower her.

Stunned stillness.

86

PART THREE

He Didn't Stand Me Up, He Said He Couldn't Stand Me

A week later. M&M's World.

RACHEL. Skincare. You think skincare will fix this?

NICK. It's just a… a gesture? I paid for it, if that helps

RACHEL.…That a dig?

NICK. No! No no… joke, meant to be a joke

RACHEL.…So… we're talking now?

NICK. You said you needed… space

RACHEL. So… talk

NICK.…Yeah okay I just wanted to say that… I do think there is good here and I don't think we need to lose that just cos…

RACHEL. Sorry – You're not going to apologise?

NICK. What? I –

RACHEL. Wow. Course, should've known

NICK. You –

RACHEL. Me? You think this is a *me* thing?

NICK. I think… No, I'm trying to say: there *is* good here and and I think things went too far, I think – there's stuff I should've communicated, said 'no' to, earlier, when I had the chance, before we –

RACHEL. And you think that's *my* fault?

NICK. Can I – I just want to – I feel kind of… used… / And I feel like you

RACHEL. Oh my God –

NICK. Took advantage of me at times and…

RACHEL. You're kidding, / you've got to be kidding

NICK. But I think we both should've gone into this with our
eyes a bit more open, had more conversations…

RACHEL. All I did to you was what *you* did to *me*

NICK. What?

RACHEL. You didn't like me being in control, you didn't like
me treating you how you treat me, that's what this is

NICK. No – that's not –

RACHEL. That's exactly –

NICK. That's ridiculous –

RACHEL. What's ridiculous is you thinking we – that there's
some kind of relationship we can scrape together out of this

NICK. But I do th–

RACHEL. Nick – I made a point of asking you to meet me in a
public place at a busy time, why do you think I did that?

NICK. Cos… We both… love M&Ms world?

RACHEL. Jesus fucking Christ you are so dumb

NICK.… So… you don't…?

RACHEL. No! Jesus! No! How can you shove me on the floor
and think I'd still – !? Even feel comfortable around you!?

NICK. I didn't – you – look, Rachel… I'm terrified of you

RACHEL. Yeah I get it I'm intimidating, I'm sick of being a
fucking *kink*

NICK. No – like – actually – *terrified*

RACHEL. What?

NICK. But I'm saying… I think we can… I think if we maybe
step away from all the… the toxicity, maybe there's –

RACHEL. Are you serious? I'm not scary, I'm not a scary
person. What, just cos I'm tall –

NICK. It's not / your height –

RACHEL. Just cos I know what I want, cos I'm direct –

NICK. It's not / that –

RACHEL. I'm not *toxic,* fuck, everyone's apparently *toxic* nowadays

NICK. Okay, okay let's pause a second, pause

It's not any of those things

RACHEL. Then what is it? Go on.

NICK. You're... hah, okay, um, this is silly but... you're like... the Mistress Twister?

They let this sink in. And then they can't help laughing cos it's so stupid.

RACHEL.... What?!!

NICK. Yeah, sorry, it's the best I could – stupid. SO stupid. But... yeah

RACHEL. Yeah, see? You've got no idea have you!? Jesus you think we have a bit of a giggle and everything's *fine*

You basically just described me as a *giant terrifying arse-busting dildo*

NICK. Okay that was stupid of me – can we please just talk this through, talk through what went wrong, what we can do better? Please!?

RACHEL. Hold on, you're saying, you're saying, what? You want to make a go of this? While you're saying you *hate* me?

NICK. I never said –

RACHEL. What's the point? If I'm such a fucking bad person?

NICK. You're not a – wait, hear me out!!!

RACHEL. No, we're done. We're done.

NICK. Please Rachel, don't do this

RACHEL. There's no Band-Aid you can just stick on this, a fucking moisturiser won't – I'm not a scary person, yeah, sure I can be – singleminded, I focused on the sex side of things too much, sure, I get that – I mean listen I have thought about it a lot this past week and, yeah, there's a major lesson to be learned here

NICK. Okay…?

Sorry, what's the lesson?

RACHEL. Well. Best not to peg

NICK.…That's… Your takeaway from all this? / THAT'S

RACHEL. Hold on –

NICK. YOUR TAKEAWAY!? PEGGING WAS THE PROBLEM? What, people shouldn't ever peg? Then everything / would be fine?!

RACHEL. Don't – don't patronise me –

NICK. PATRONISE *YOU*?!! ARE YOU KIDDING ME!!!

RACHEL. You're – you're starting to scare me now –

NICK. YEAH! THAT'D MAKE TWO OF US! JESUS FUCKING CHRIST. Oh my God, 'best not to peg' am I like am I in a parallel universe?

Is that it? That's the big epiphany?

RACHEL. *You* wanted to talk it through, I'm talking it through!

NICK. I wanted *you*, Rachel, just you, sex aside, costumes aside, frills aside, bullshit aside, lights on, eye to eye, warts and all, just *you*.

And you lost your fucking mind when I asked you for that

And you made me feel *this* big. And *you* haven't apologised yet.

RACHEL.…I was drunk

NICK. Oh come ON – 'Best not to peg', sorry, I just cannot get over that

RACHEL. Don't make fun of me

NICK. BEST NOT TO PEG, I'm sorry it's the funniest things you've ever said

RACHEL. YOU CALLED ME THE MISTRESS TWISTER

NICK. YOU FUCKING ARE! You're a fucking… bully! And we know why bullies pick on other kids, don't we?

RACHEL. YOU'RE – you know what

What was her name? The girl you kissed?

Did she, what, kiss you on the forehead? Call you a 'good boy'?

NICK. …How –

RACHEL. Yeah, I heard you and Eddie at the wedding, you little bitch

He puts his head in his hands, upset.

She laughs, contemptuously.

You honestly give me, this, like, emotional *ick*, you know that?

You're all the same. You're all the fucking same.

NICK. You fight so dirty, you know that?

RACHEL. Used to turn you on

NICK. Yeah, when it was make-believe. Not *all the fucking time*.

RACHEL. You want the good, the bad and the ugly, here it is, babe. Here it is.

NICK. …It was an accident

RACHEL. You accidentally popped your tongue in her mouth?

NICK. You know, Rachel… There's ugly, and there's *ugly*. And you're *ugly*. I'm out, I'm fucking –

RACHEL. YOU don't get to break up with ME – YOU DON'T GET TO –

NICK. 'Best not to peg' – honestly? You can suck a bag of dicks, don't contact me again.

I Am Totally Fine (Except for the Tornado of Rage Inside of Me)

Winter.

To us:

RACHEL. I get on the apps. All of them. They give me the semblance of control over my dating life that I need, even though each and every one of them is a raging hellscape.

NICK. I scroll instagram. I go on Snapchat. I watch YouTube videos on how to make perfect ramen. I clean my house. I watch *Bojack Horseman*. I read some articles about crypto but I still don't understand it. I do pull-ups. Drink water. Do some work. Play chess. Play Fifa. Watch *Succession*. I check instagram again but I don't check Rachel's profile, I don't watch her stories, I watch videos of CEOs talking about leadership.

I have recurring dreams about being falsely imprisoned for something I didn't do.

RACHEL *scrolls*.

RACHEL. No no no no no no no no no no, basic, no no no no no no, drugged tiger picture, no no no no no no no

Hobbies – food, nights out, TRAVELLING!

'I'm looking for someone to go on adventures with.'

Travelling. Is not. A personality trait. NAME ME ONE PERSON WHO DOESN'T LIKE GOING ON HOLIDAY?

'Just looking for someone who doesn't take life too seriously!'

You know what? I TAKE LIFE SERIOUSLY. Look around, everything's on fire! LIVING IS A SERIOUS BUSINESS

I don't say that, I send a peach emoji.

NICK. I do… a lot of cocaine

RACHEL. I get a new job. At a big marketing agency. Like, a big-dick job. Great salary, free lunches, office gym. And I'm living in East London now, with three twenty-four year old Gen Z-ers.

I make a point of posting stories of me having a ball – pictures of bonfire night, mulled wine, Christmas markets. Just so he knows, I am having the time of my life.

Cos I know he's looking, I know he's looking.

NICK. I've blocked her on all platforms.

RACHEL. I go silent speed-dating. Yes: SILENT SPEED-DATING. I saw it on *Time Out*, an article about quirky dating and ways to meet people, and I'm a millennial whose entire personality is based on dating horror stories and tales of woe, so I of course buy a ticket. And basically, what you do is, just stare at each other. Stare into each other's souls. I hate it here, I hate these people.

NICK. More cocaine, can't get enough cocaine. I am also going to the gym more though, shredding, so, you know, cancels out.

RACHEL. I go to a 'wedding-themed' dating night. Yeah.

I'm en route, literally on the tram to South Croydon when Fiona bails on me, saying she needs to 'immerse herself in a self-care cocoon this evening'.

I'm going to a wedding-themed dating night. On my own.

We're all given characters. I'm the sister-in-law. I'm having a quiet smoke outside when I get chatting to a guy – comedian – playing the best man. He's wearing a suit jacket over a pair of crusty jogging bottoms, and brought his own Sainsbury's 'for life' bag with tinnies in.

I stick with him because I don't know anyone else here and I hate that I'm here. I hate it. New years eve's a few weeks away, so I ask him what his hopes and dreams are – for next year – and he says: he doesn't have any.

Then he lunges to kiss me and I swerve and I'm, like, really pissed off – like *how* did he think, just cos I'm standing near him, *how* did this despondent, failed comic think this could possibly be a thing?

NICK. Worried I might die from all the cocaine, but that's not gonna stop me

RACHEL. I text Fiona, see if she wants to go for drinks. She doesn't reply for days.

NICK. Eddie attempts an intervention and I tell him to go fuck himself.

RACHEL. Then I get a long WhatsApp that says:

'After a difficult year, personally, I am currently on a healing journey and trying to create healthy boundaries and honour my needs throughout this process. As my nervous system is quite dysregulated at the moment, I don't currently have the capacity to hold space for you. I find your negativity at times quite triggering and so, for now, I am keeping my circle to a few close friends whom I feel safe with. The season of our friendship has been nourishing, but our paths must now diverge. I wish you the very best on your own journey and hope you find the support you so need. Please respect my boundaries and do not reach out to me again. Oh, and Merry Christmas. Regards, Fiona.'

NICK. I didn't get the contract in the end. Manager said I'd taken my eye off the ball. I was too… passive.

RACHEL. January. I turn up for a date off an app with a guy in a Barbour jacket. First red flag.

NICK. I do meet a girl at the gym: Dana. Proper… yoga instructor body. From Spain. She's… nice

RACHEL. And it turns out… He is OBSESSED with pegging, like, his biggest kink. Brings it up, unprompted – as if he saw me walk in and was like 'THANK YOU GOD FOR SENDING ME THIS GIANT LADY TO DESTROY MY ARSEHOLE'

So I do. I destroy it.

NICK. And we start sleeping together. And that's nice. She's nice to me. She actually kisses me

RACHEL. The next time I see him, we're walking to the Tube and he asks if I can hold his hand, you know, like, the other way around, so he's like 'the girl'. And yeah, it disgusts me a bit, but I do it, cos that's what you do for someone.

NICK. She's nice – no, not nice, not just nice – kind. She's kind. She buys me treats. Asks how my day was. Seems to be into straightforward, normal, perfunctory, no frills sex.

RACHEL. We go on a few dates but, to be honest, he becomes a bit of a stuck record, he's just so delighted he found this… giant pegging lady. But he never like, asks me any questions.

NICK. Asks about my baggage. Exes. So I tell her, yeah, cliche but… I do have a crazy ex-girlfriend. She tells me that's a red flag and she has to think about it. Few days later, we pick things up. But I think what's bothering me is –

RACHEL. But I think the thing is, the thing that's *really* turning me off is… / He's *boring*

NICK. Is she… boring?

RACHEL. I text / him

NICK. Fuck, she texts me

RACHEL. Hey

NICK. Ignore it

RACHEL. Hey, WYD?

NICK. Nope

RACHEL. For fuck's – HEY

NICK. I throw my phone out the window. It lands by the bins and in three seconds some kid's run over, grabbed it, and legged it.

RACHEL. I decide I'm going to be alone. It's good for me to be alone. Don't need a man. Don't need anyone. If I'm too much, go find less, you know?

My Heart Attacks

NICK. I call them my heart attacks but I don't really know what
they are. It's like a squeezing with an injection of adrenaline.
Sometimes it's my heart like adding beats, like boom-ba-ba-
ba-ba-ba-boom and I've got to catch my breath – whatever
it is, I didn't used to have it before and now it's every other
day, more. Maybe it's in the air. Maybe it's the weather.
Maybe it's the pace of life. Maybe it's breathing in that black
soot everyday on the Tube. Maybe it's commuting. Maybe
it's the cultural consciousness. Maybe it's being a millennial.
Maybe it's the climate crisis. Maybe it's the patriarchy. Pret
A Manger. Plants. Plantain. I've got no idea. And I've had
this headache for three days now. I can't sleep. I'm exhausted
but when I go to bed – when I've been desperate to get to bed
all day, there's a fizzing behind my eyes. Wired. I almost feel
more awake. I feel like the walking dead every day. Like it's
mercury or cold metal going up and down my veins. I think
obsessively about stealing stationery at work. I think about
punching my boss, I don't know why I just picture blood
coming out of his nose. I work out til I rip muscles. My
heart's still going, I feel it pounding like it's trying to bust out
of my chest. I want to dig it out with a carving knife. I want
to be free. I want to be at peace. I want my dad. I want my
mum. I want to think about other things – or nothing at all. I
stand on the Tube platform and sometimes when the train's
coming I think about jumping, I don't want to jump, I just
think I could jump, but everyone thinks that right? I think of
all the bad things I've done. I think of all the bad decisions
I've made. Dead. I'm dead. That's the word that intrudes
dead dead dead dead dead. I should be dead. Not in a suicide
way but just dead. I repeat it and it blocks out the sound of
all the guilt and constant recurring thoughts about being a
bad person. I'm not a bad person. I've done nothing wrong.
Whatever. I don't want to think any more.

I've Never Seen Trash Take Itself Out

RACHEL. I hate men. I do. I hate how basic they are. I
    hate how stupid they are. I hate how they think they own
    everything. I hate how they think the world is fair only cos
    it's fair to them. I hate how all of them need parenting, no
    matter what age they are. I hate that they think women can
    only be one thing. I hate that they don't care if we enjoy
    sex or not. I hate that most of them don't know how to help
    a woman enjoy sex. I hate how when they're older their
    guts spill over the top of their trousers and they wear their
    belt underneath it. I hate how they spread their legs on the
    Tube. I hate how they don't even realise how their eyes
    scan us on the street. I hate how they get to hold a stare
    but if we look back they're stupid enough to think we're
    soliciting. I hate how they'll have sex with anything. I hate
    this idea they have that women can have sex at any time,
    that we're the gatekeepers and it's about banging down the
    door til you get in. I hate how they call us emotional like
    it's a bad thing. I hate how emotionally stunted they all are.
    I hate that they treat women like therapists and emotional
    rehabilitation centres. I hate how they take over the weights
    section at the gym. I hate how they put their hands on your
    waist to move past you at the bar. I hate how they baulk if
    you are direct with them. I hate laughing at their shit jokes.
    I hate smiling. I hate when they can't accept I'm funnier
    and smarter than them. I hate how they think women aren't
    funny. I hate how they call grown women 'girls'. I hate how
    men have no idea how we behave when they're not there.
    We're not afraid to get our tits out. Be naked. Let our fat roll
    and roll. I hate that they don't know what consent is. I hate
    that a no is a yes-in-waiting to them. I hate that they don't
    want to wear condoms and we have to torture our bodies
    on the pill. I hate that they're afraid of us. I hate that they
    get six-month jail sentences for raping us because they're
    good swimmers. I hate that they legislate on our bodies. I
    hate that they hire their friends and fire women for getting
    pregnant – conveniently forgetting they play a part in making

those same pregnancies happen. I hate the way small men insist on dating smaller women. I hate the way they want sex at all times but no sluts. I hate the way they're all into choking now. I hate that they ghost you. I hate that it's an unspoken, but known, thing that they all watch violent porn. I hate that they send us dick pics. I hate that they traffick women. I hate that they hit women. I hate that they make US out to be the irrational ones. I hate that they take classes on how to sleep with us. I hate that they all want a woman half their age. I hate that they date younger women because they know they're more compliant – because they've jaded the rest of us – we're wise to them. I hate that they'll sleep with underage girls and say they didn't realise. I hate that they kiss their mothers with the same mouths with which they spit on us. I hate that the waiter assumes the wine is for the woman and the beer for men. I hate that they all think they could beat Serena Williams at tennis. I hate that fathers give brides away. I hate that young girls are exploited in abuse rings and ALL the men involved clearly have no issue with it. I hate men who say 'not all men' but also have that friend they think assaulted someone but don't want to rock the boat by calling them out, so continue to be friends with him. I hate that they think we're less than human: that they have thoughts, dreams, angst, pain, woe and they think we don't – that ours is less. I hate that Chris Brown still has a career and a willing audience. I hate that they don't understand periods. I hate that they stone us to death. I hate that they follow us. I hate that they stalk us. I hate that they threaten us. I hate how much space they take up. I hate that they use the simple fact that they're bigger to keep us in place. I hate that they expect less of us. I hate that they think women's sport is shit. I hate that they can't handle being 'beaten by a girl.' I hate that they aren't fighting for equality. I hate that they don't like body hair. I hate that they post videos and photos of us online and to their friends. I hate that their trousers have pockets and ours don't. I hate that they go bald. I hate that they think make-up is silly when actually it's art. I hate when they say feminists are ugly. I hate incels. I hate that they think lesbian sex is for them. I hate that they whistle at us. I hate that they

shout from building sites. I hate that they never queue for
the loo. That the world is designed for them from phones to
crash dummies and we die because of it. I hate that they go
to strip clubs for work or with their friends. I hate that they
excuse it or say 'That's just how it is' – or – 'She was alright
with it, she wouldn't be doing it otherwise, would she?' I
hate that they worry about their teenage daughters cos they
know what they were like when they were young. I hate
that they'd date someone else's teenage daughter. I hate that
rape is a weapon of war. I hate that virginity is a thing. I hate
that 'strong women' is a genre and suggests therefore that,
as a default, all women are weak. I hate that it's not okay to
be weak. I hate that they create hostile working conditions
and punish us for not meeting the 'bar'. I hate that the bar
is male. I hate that kindness is weakness. That vulnerability
is weakness. I hate how their come tastes. I hate that they're
afraid of being feminine. I hate that they use 'girl' as an
insult. I hate that they circumcise young girls. I hate that they
run governments – badly. I hate that they join the Bullingdon
Club then become PM. I hate that they think it was all down
to their hard work. I hate that childcare is solely a women's
issue.

I will not be told I'm wrong.

I hate 'nice guys' who are actually not nice at all. I hate
men who claim they're feminists to sleep with women. I
hate men who say they're feminists but talk over women
and lecture them about being bad feminists. I hate men who
can't see the women in their lives bending over backwards to
make things easier for them. I hate men who grope women
in the street, in bars and at work. I hate men who use their
power to coerce women into sex. I hate men who withhold
promotions and career progression for women until they
receive sexual favours – and then say those same women
slept their way to the top. I hate men who don't mind having
sex with women who don't want to fuck them. I hate men
who wank into pot plants. I hate men who leer. I hate men
who impregnate women then cheat on them or leave them. I
hate men who think single mothers are the scourge of society.

I hate men who only talk about themselves. I hate men who boast about how much money they have. I hate men who ask their girlfriends to go on Tinder to find a woman to have a threesome with. I hate men who'd have a threesome with another woman but never another man. I hate men who wear gilets. I hate old drunk men who hit on you in bars but I hate *more* that they live in a world where they think they have a chance. I hate men who don't know what they want. I hate men who don't make the first move. I hate men who think women shouldn't be too keen or make the first move. I hate men who chase sex then go off the girl when they get it cos she 'put out'. I hate men who burn witches. I hate men who make women feel insecure about their bodies. I hate men who do it on purpose to 'neg' them into sex. I hate men who make women feel insecure about their vaginas and how they smell. I hate men who date good-looking women for status, to say, 'I am capable and worthy of this – me – me – look at what I can get – I must be a top quality person.' I hate men who tell women not to breastfeed in public. I hate men who tell women to quiet their babies down in public. I hate men who call women feminazis. I hate men who design toilets out of trains because they forgot to think about how women might need the bathroom more because our bodies are different. I hate men who vote to keep a luxury tax on tampons. I hate men who interrupt the intense conversation you're having with your girl pal who you've not seen in six months and just want to spend time with, then get affronted when you don't want to chat. I hate men who steal our ideas. I hate men who think the only reason you are turning them down must be because you are taken, owned by another man, not that you're simply NOT INTERESTED. I hate men who flash young girls. I hate men who expose themselves to women on the bus. I hate men who get on packed Tubes to sexually harass trapped women. I hate men who tell women it's hysteria when they're actually having heart attacks. I hate men who tell women to calm down.

I think I'm done

I don't feel any better.

NICK. I take the plunge. I post a picture of me and Dana at a picnic on my Instagram. Feed, not stories.

Pause. RACHEL *takes this in.*

RACHEL. It's of both of them crying with laughter.

My dad calls, again. I let it ring out, so then he texts me: 'I'm off the drink. For good. Will you come see your old man?'

You Pegged My Soul

To us:

RACHEL. I get a message from Eddie, which is EXTREMELY creepy because I don't know how he got my number, but it also tracks. He says it's a shame not to have seen me in a while, hopes I'm okay, and he wondered if I can come pick up some of my stuff cos it's cluttering their flat?

So, yeah, I go, whatever, he tells me not to worry, Nick will be out, it's all bagged up, okay, so I arrive and I'm about to be like, 'Where's my fucking stuff Eddie?' cos I can't see anything, and he like, ushers – kind of pushes – me into his bedroom and I'm like, right, okay, this is it, you always knew this is on the cards, Eddie's decided to strangle you, chop you up and pickle your body parts –

NICK. What the / fuck –

RACHEL. What the fuck – the door slams behind me –

NICK. What the fuck – he locks it

RACHEL. What the fuck – Eddie's – oh / my God

NICK. Oh my God he didn't – Eddie!? / EDDIE?

RACHEL. EDDIE?!!

NICK. EDDIE WHAT THE FUCK IS GOING ON?

RACHEL. EDDIE I AM GOING TO MURDER YOU, I WILL
MURDER –

NICK. EDDIE YOU SAID YOU WERE GOING TO SHOW
ME YOUR NEW NAZGUL WARHAMMER –

Both take turns to play Eddie:

RACHEL. THIS IS MY LAST ATTEMPT!

NICK. I HAVE TRIED AN INTERVENTION!

RACHEL. I HAVE TRIED LENDING YOU SELF-HELP
BOOKS –

NICK. SHOWING YOU THERAPY TIKTOKS –

RACHEL. AND I HAVE TRIED EMOTIONALLY
WITHDRAWING IN THE HOPES THAT YOU'D NOTICE
SOMETHING WAS WRONG AND TRY AND HAVE AN
ACTUAL CONVERSATION FOR ONCE

NICK. BUT YOUR HEAD'S *SO* FAR UP YOUR OWN
ARSEHOLE YOU DIDN'T EVEN NOTICE, YOU JUST
DID SO MUCH COKE IT'D BRING PABLO-FUCKING-
ESCOBAR TO TEARS

RACHEL. RACHEL, HE'S ON YOUR INSTAGRAM
FOURTEEN HOURS A DAY

As himself:

NICK. That's not true

As Eddie:

RACHEL. AND I KNOW IT'S NOT FAIR ON YOU COS
WOMEN ARE *NOT* EMOTIONAL REHABILITATION
CENTRES FOR MEN BUT I AM HONESTLY AT MY
WITS END

NICK. PLEASE JUST SORT IT OUT, GET BACK
TOGETHER, GO TO THERAPY, SOMETHING, I'M SICK
TO THE BACK TEETH OF IT I CAN'T LIVE WITH THIS
EMOTIONAL BABY-MAN, I CAN'T

I'M GOING OUT NOW, I'LL BE BACK IN A BIT

They look at each other.

RACHEL. EDDIE?!!

NICK. EDDIE?!!

RACHEL. FUCK YOU EDDIE, LET ME OUT

NICK. FUCK YOU! FUCK YOU EDDIE

RACHEL. FUCK YOU

But he's gone.

RACHEL *and* NICK *look at each other.*

What is... / What the

NICK. I don't look at your Instagram. I don't.

Silence.

RACHEL. So many Beanie Babies

NICK. He made bread and butter pudding, he lured me in here with bread and butter pudding

Disbelief.

NICK *eats the pudding.*

It's delicious

RACHEL. Soggy

Silence.

...*Are* you okay?

NICK. I'm fine. Never better. I don't know what he's on about, seriously, never better. You?

RACHEL. Thriving. EDDIE?

NICK. EDDIE!?!?!?

RACHEL. EDDIE?

NICK. What a prick

RACHEL. What a cunt

NICK. Sorry about this I had no idea he –

RACHEL. Oh – ha – refreshing

NICK. Huh?

RACHEL. To hear you say sorry

NICK. Not the time

RACHEL. Literally is the time

NICK. Over my dead body

RACHEL. Don't tempt me I'm *this* close to a double homicide

Silence.

NICK. Oh fuck

RACHEL. What

NICK. No I'm just – I know where this [has come from] – I was uh high the other night, and I was [telling him]… I actually ended up telling him about… everything, the breakup, the pegging, even –

RACHEL. Really?!

NICK. I needed to just, get it off my chest

RACHEL. How'd he take it?

NICK. I mean, hilariously, he was just like, 'Yeah, cool. Everybody's got a thing, I guess… I'm quite into feet actually'

RACHEL. Fuck noooooooooo

NICK. Yeah

RACHEL. Noooooo!!! I always thought he was really boring

NICK. He is boring, that's the thing, he is

He was actually really good about it all, to be fair to him. And I think I have been a bit of a nightmare… if I'm honest

RACHEL. You do look like shit

NICK. Thanks, so do you

RACHEL. Cheers

Silence.

I um...

I went to see my dad yesterday.

NICK. Really? How was it?

RACHEL. It was um, it was okay actually. He says he's off the drink.

NICK. Oh yeah? I mean... that's good? Do you... believe him?

RACHEL. ...Um... I think... I'm choosing to.

We've been here before but... yeah, I'm choosing to.

NICK. Did he say why?

RACHEL. Went into work steaming. Pissed himself.

NICK. Christ...

RACHEL. In front of everyone, his boss. Lost his job. Again.

He said... This is why I do think... he said, he doesn't want to be ashamed anymore.

Silence.

NICK. I really hope he gets better.

RACHEL. Thank you.

I'm... tired. I'm tired of being angry all the time.

NICK. Ha, yeah [same]

RACHEL. What's wrong with me? There's something wrong, isn't there?

And even now, even now I would happily steal Eddie's holographic Charizard, just to teach him a lesson

NICK. Ahhhhhahahahaaaaa

She goes to take a water bottle out of her bag. NICK *visibly flinches*

RACHEL. OhmyGod don't worry it's… Look, water. Not a –

NICK. Thank God, *thank God*

RACHEL. Christ, I'm a monster, aren't I?

Pause.

NICK. Eddie um, he really pulled me up on the…The kiss – the cheating.

I knew what I was doing, I knew it would destroy you, and did it anyway, at the time I felt like it was the only power I had, but that doesn't excuse it, and you didn't deserve that, you deserved better.

I'm sorry for cheating on you.

RACHEL. It's really heartening that you wouldn't listen to me but you were willing to listen to another man

NICK. I didn't [only listen to another man] – right… okay, yeah… fair

RACHEL. But thank you.

NICK. Okay.

And – you're not a giant arse-busting dildo, you're much better looking.

Beat.

RACHEL. I'm sorry –

NICK. Thank you

RACHEL. That your housemate's such a dong

NICK. Oh for –

RACHEL. I'm joking, I am actually really sorry.

That I put all that on you

NICK....Thank you

Hopeful silence... Has Eddie heard?

I think he has actually gone out

RACHEL. Balls

NICK. Try the pudding

RACHEL. Absolutely not

NICK. He made custard from scratch

RACHEL. Grow up

Silence.

It's like... I... pegged your butt... but you pegged... my soul?

NICK. FUCK! So silly!

RACHEL. So silly, I know

NICK. You were sitting on that one weren't you

RACHEL. Oh for ages

Silence.

NICK. You know when your dad – he was talking about like, an arts...

RACHEL. Oh

NICK. Music school ...? What was your... was it singing or an instrument or

RACHEL. No, I can't tell you

NICK. Why not?

RACHEL. No – cos you'll laugh

NICK. Okay, you have to now

RACHEL. No, seriously

NICK. Tell, tell, tell, tell –

RACHEL. Oh my fucking / God –

NICK. TELL TELL TELL TELL –

RACHEL. Trombone! Okay? Trombone!

NICK. No.

　No, you're joking

RACHEL. Nope, no joke

NICK. No… You played the –

RACHEL. Don't make the joke, I can feel it on the tip of your tongue, don't make the joke –

NICK. I have to

RACHEL. Don't, you're above that, don't do it, force it down, crush it down.

　He does.

　I was really good at it as well

　They giggle.

　Silence.

　…Do you think there's a world in which… We…

NICK. Do *you* think that's a good idea?

RACHEL.…Um… no

NICK. Yeah

RACHEL. Yeah

　Friends, even?

NICK. Um… no

RACHEL. Okay

NICK. Yeah

RACHEL.…Send you memes occasionally?

NICK. Uhhhhhh […maybe?] …no.

　Silence.

RACHEL. I *do* think it's best not to peg

They crack up, too hard, until it's kind of sad?

You have to laugh, don't you?

NICK. You really, really do.

RACHEL. We're broken aren't we?

NICK. Oh we're fucked

Silence.

You're not a bad person. Rachel.

RACHEL. ...Do you mean that?

Like, how do I actually...?

NICK. ...Hah, okay, you know what you should do?

RACHEL. Peg the pain away?

NICK. Ha, no.

RACHEL. Go on...

NICK. Give Monika back her Tupperware.

RACHEL. Oh wow. Wow. Woooooooow.

I've stopped drinking and smoking. I've taken up yoga.
I even did a Google search for therapists in my area. I'm
willing to undergo profound personal and spiritual growth.
What I'm saying is, I hear you, but I will not give up the
Tupperware.

NICK. Think about it.

RACHEL. No. Fine. No.

Maybe.

Curtain.

A Nick Hern Book

The Misandrist first published in Great Britain as a paperback original in 2023 by Nick Hern Books Limited, The Glasshouse, 49a Goldhawk Road, London W12 8QP, in association with Metal Rabbit Productions

The Misandrist copyright © 2023 Lisa Carroll

Lisa Carroll has asserted her right to be identified as the author of this work

Cover design by Michael Wharley / DeskTidy

Designed and typeset by Nick Hern Books, London
Printed in Great Britain by Mimeo Ltd, Huntingdon, Cambridgeshire PE29 6XX

A CIP catalogue record for this book is available from the British Library

ISBN 978 1 83904 219 5

Performing Rights   Applications for performance, including readings and excerpts, in the English language throughout the world should be addressed in the first instance to the Performing Rights Department, Nick Hern Books, The Glasshouse, 49a Goldhawk Road, London W12 8QP, *tel* +44 (0)20 8749 4953, *email* rights@nickhernbooks.co.uk, except as follows:

Australia: ORiGiN Theatrical, Level 1, 213 Clarence Street, Sydney NSW 2000, *tel* +61 (2) 8514 5201, *email* enquiries@originmusic.com.au, *web* www.origintheatrical.com.au

New Zealand: Play Bureau, 20 Rua Street, Mangapapa, Gisborne 4010, *tel* +64 21 258 3998, *email* info@playbureau.com

No performance of any kind may be given unless a licence has been obtained. Applications should be made before rehearsals begin. Publication of this play does not necessarily indicate its availability for amateur performance.

Woodland CARBON
www.woodlandcarbon.co.uk
NICK HERN BOOKS
Printed on Carbon Captured paper